Horizons Penmanship

Teacher's Guide

Author:
Mary Ellen Quint, Ph.D.
Editor:
Alan Christopherson, M.S.

Alpha Omega Publications, Inc. • Rock Rapids, IA

Alpha Omega Publications, Inc.
804 N. 2nd Ave. E.
Rock Rapids, IA 51246-1759

Printed in the United States of America

ISBN 978-0-7403-0206-0

Table of Contents

Introduction

Introduction

"Whatever you do, work at it with all your heart, as working for the Lord, not for men." (Colossians 3:23).

Good handwriting is a necessary skill in life.

All too often in our modern times good penmanship is neglected. Many children and adults rely on computers for the bulk of their writing, but the ability to fill in a form, to write a card of congratulations or sympathy, to write a personal letter to a friend or to add a personal touch to messages is important. Computers fail at times — the ability to write does not.

Handwriting is important.

Like riding a bicycle or developing any other skill, handwriting must be learned through consistent practice. Often in crowded schedules, it is left out of the curriculum, used simply as "busy work" or given too short a time period to be effective.

Handwriting time should be a relaxed time, not a stressful time.

Always give adequate "warm-up" time before writing, especially in the beginning when children are learning the formation of new letters. Have them form letters in the air, on their desks, etc., as an introductory activity each day until they are sure of the letter formations and the correct starting and ending points. After doing some initial warm-up exercises, try adding some soft, light classical music in the background while the children practice.

Keep it short.

The total time for handwriting class should not be more than 10–15 minutes at one sitting. Children will tire, and they will not be able to do their best. Teach the children simple hand exercises to use (shaking the hands, moving them around) if they get tired.

Always be positive.

Circle and comment on well-made letters rather than on errors. Even if the entire page is a problem, find the one letter that is the closest to being correct and use that as an example.

Practice is important.

Reproducible practice pages are included in the handbook. These may be copied to use with children who need extra practice and to make a practice copy of the Bible verse.

Stress the importance of doing ALL things well for God.

Emphasize the fact that rushing through a lesson without doing one's best does not praise God and will not lead to good writing habits. Remind the children that writing is a means of communication with others. If their writing cannot be read, then their message will never be understood.

Pre-writing

1. To assess the level of the children, give each a piece of lined paper (you may use the reproducible master in the back of the *Teacher's Guide*) and have them write their name and any letters or words they may know. This will not be graded but will give you an idea of how much practice the children have had in writing. It will also give you a page with which to compare progress at the end of the semester or school year.
2. Print each child's name on a strip of tag board and laminate it if possible. Have it before the child for reference at all times.
3. Have a classroom alphabet chart and individual letter cards displayed in the classroom. You may also want to copy and laminate the small chart in the student book for use on an individual basis at the child's desk.

Excerpts from Student Book Pages

The following pages are taken from the portion of the student book that covers hand and paper position, posture, spacing, placement, and letter formation. They are included in the *Teacher's Guide* for your reference.

Hand, Pencil, and Posture Positions (page 4)

Look at each picture with the children and have them model the correct position. Ask the children to tell which hand they use to write. Have them find the picture they will use as a model. Check both right- and left-handed positions. Watch the left-handed child carefully so that he or she does not slant the paper on the wrong angle and try to use a "hooked" hand position.

Correct Spacing (page 5)

Have the children raise the index (pointer) finger of the hand they will NOT use for writing. Demonstrate how they can use that finger to see how much space they will need between individual letters for practice and, later, between words.

Rocket (page 5)

Discuss the rocket and its parts. Using the alphabet chart for the classroom, have the children look at the letters and tell which sections of the rocket will be used for each letter. You may want to group them in categories: letters using only one section of the rocket (booster); letters using two sections of the rocket (second stage and booster OR booster and tail). Do this over several days for a few minutes each day so that the children become accustomed to using the rocket as a reference if they forget how to form a letter.

Manuscript Letters and Numbers (page 6)

This will be the reference chart for the children when they begin to write their letters. You may want to remove it from the student book and laminate it as a desk reference to be kept in the child's writing folder.

Weekly Bible Verse (page 7)

This page is a look at the Bible verse pages the children will be using beginning in the eighth week (Lessons 36–40). Read the page with the children. Look at the sample practice page which shows the "layout" of the verse. Look at the special page they will use to make their own copy of the verse to share with someone. For students who need additional practice, reproducible masters for each Bible verse page are in the back of the *Teacher's Guide*. Talk about sharing God's Word with others. Stress the importance of being able to write to others about God and to be able to share His Word with them. Discuss ways in which the special pages can be used.

From the student book...

Correct Right-Handed Position

Paper is placed on an angle to the left. Left hand steadies the paper and moves it up as you near the bottom of the page. Right hand is free to write.

Correct Left-Handed Position

Paper is placed on an angle to the right. Right hand steadies the paper and moves it up as you near the bottom of the page. Left hand is free to write. Watch hand positions carefully as shown in the picture.

Correct Hand and Pencil Position

Hold the pencil loosely about 1/2" to 1" above the sharpened point. Hold it between your thumb and index (pointer) finger. Let it rest on your middle finger. Do not grip the pencil tightly or your hand will become very tired. Do not let your hand slip down to the sharp point or you will have difficulty writing properly.

Correct Posture

Sit up tall, leaning slightly forward but not bending over your desk. Have your feet flat on the floor. Both arms will rest on the desk. Hold the paper with your free hand.

From the student book...

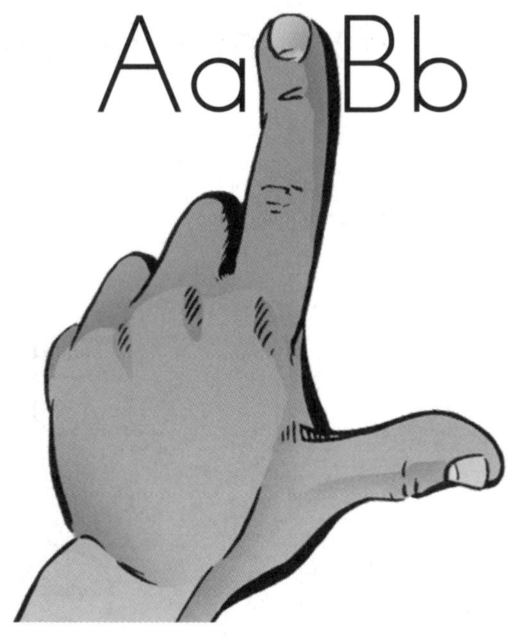

Correct Spacing

When practicing your letters separately and, later, when writing your words, use your index (pointer) finger as a guide. Continue to do this until you can easily see the space you need between words without using your finger.

Rocket Guide

The rocket will be your guide to learning your letter formations. All letters will fit into the rocket ship. Some will begin at the top of the second stage. Some will begin at the dotted line that starts the booster. Some will even move down into the tail. Look at your alphabet chart and see where the letters will fit into the rocket.

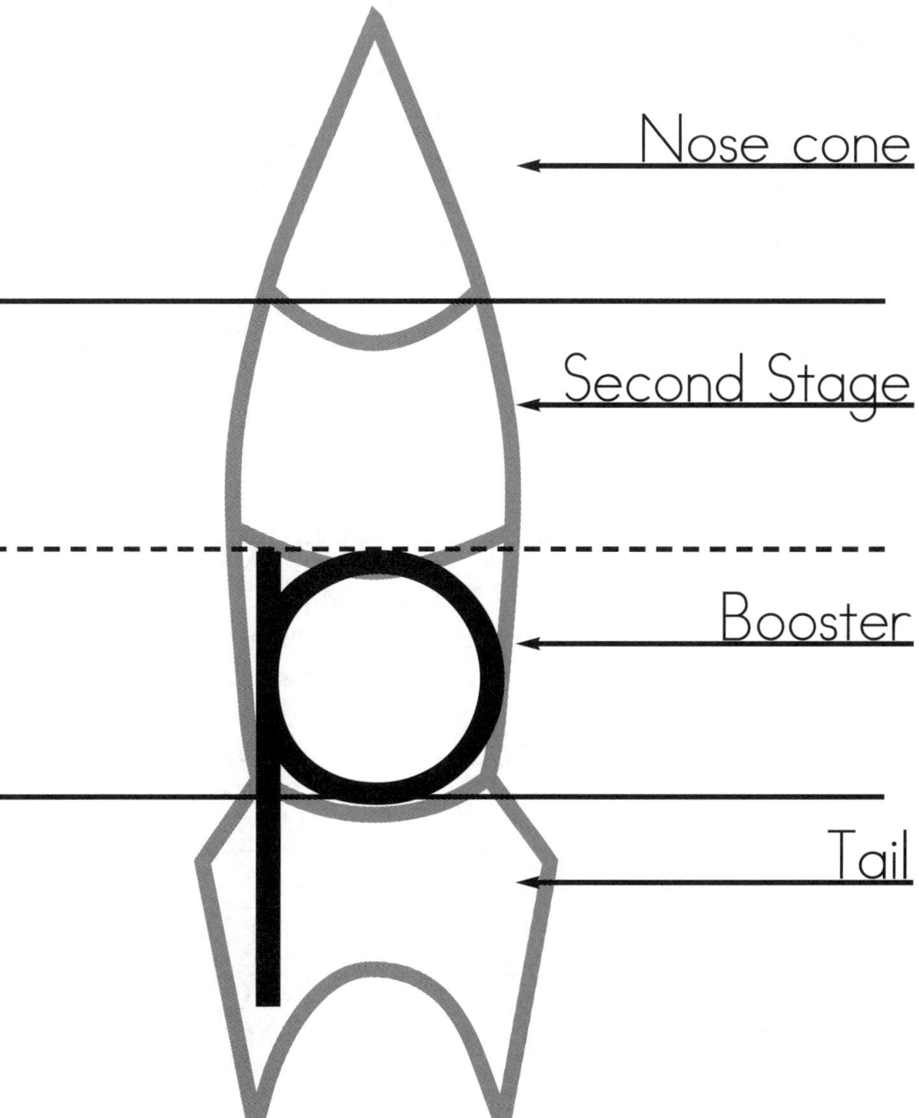

From the student book...

Correct Formation of Manuscript Letters and Numbers

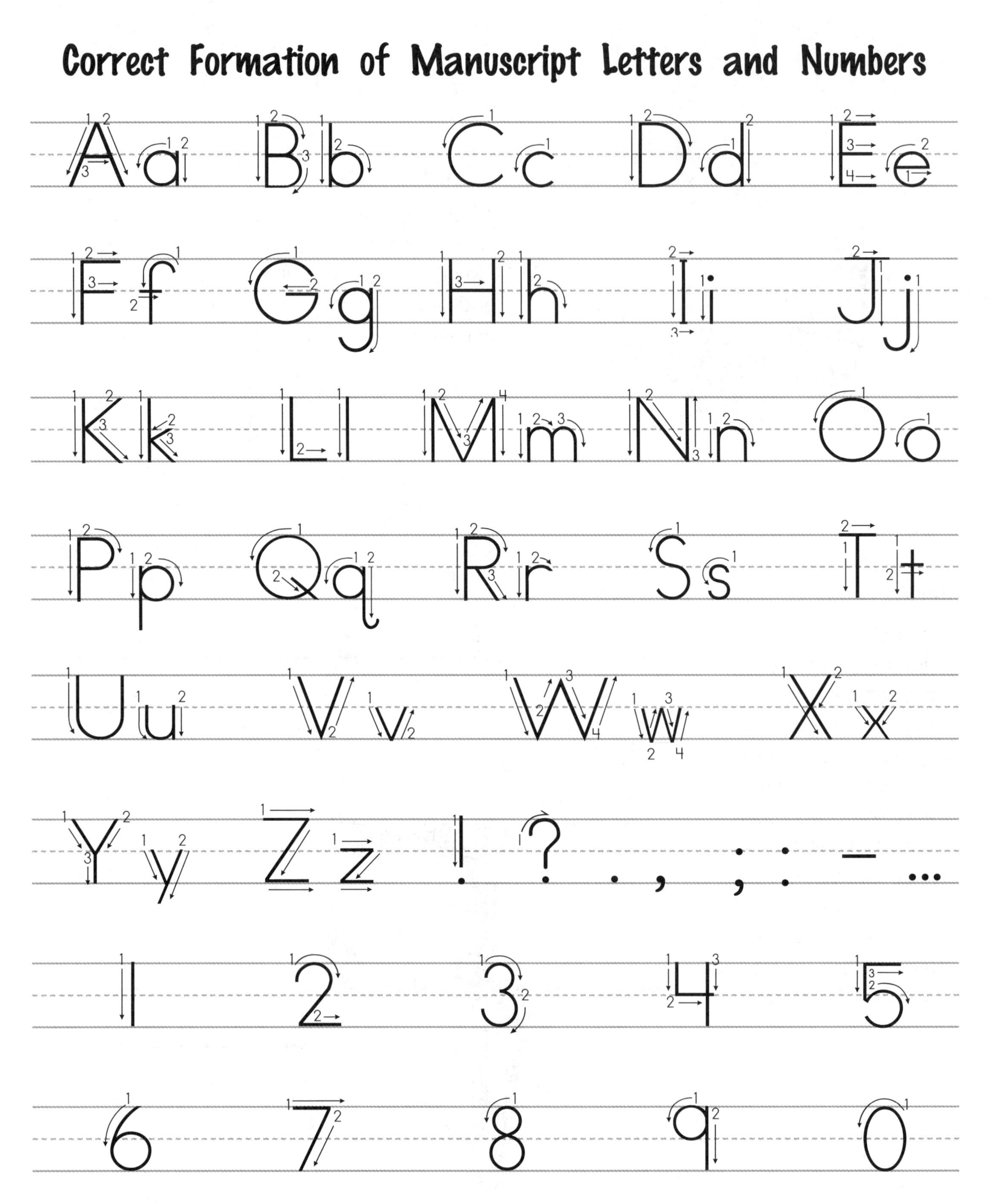

From the student book...

Lesson 69 Name:

Glory to God in the highest, and on earth peace to men on whom His favor rests.

Luke 2:14

Glory to God in the highest, and on earth peace to men on whom His favor rests.

Luke 2:14

Horizons

88

One very special thing you can do once you have learned to write is to share God's Word with others.

Beginning with Lesson 36, you will have your own special Bible verse for each week. After practicing the letters and words needed for the verse for three days, you will be able to practice your verse on the fourth day.

Lesson 70 Name:

Horizons Penmanship Grade One

89

You will also have a special page on the fifth day of the week where you will copy the verse, decorate it, and decide how you will share it with someone else.

Talk with your teacher and classmates about how you might share these special pages and share God's Word.

Scope & Sequence

Scope & Sequence

Lesson 1 *Circle practice.* Full page with line for child's first name. (NOTE: Weeks 1–5 child will write first name only. Weeks 6–32 first and last name. Child will practice drawing circles on a picture with several circular objects for student to trace.

Lesson 2 *Circle practice.* Full page with line for child's name.

Lesson 3 *Circle practice.* On template lines.

Lines 1, 2, 3: large, broken-line circles to be traced – **X** or arrow at 2:00 starting position.

Lines 4, 5, 6: small, broken-line circles to be traced.

Lesson 4 *Circle practice.* Half page – the box is for the child to draw their own freehand circle picture. The two practice lines include first line with large and small *solid* circles and second line with large and small broken-line circles.

Lesson 5 *Circle practice.* Six lines for writing.

Lines 1 & 2: Broken O (three on a line) and the child will finish the line.

Lines 3 & 4: Broken o (three on a line) and the child will finish the line.

Line 5: Broken O o

Line 6: O o – child finishes line.

Lesson 6 *Line identification & tracing:* | = red / = blue \ = green

Lesson 7 *Line tracing.* Six lines for writing.

Lines 1 & 2: Solid & broken |

Lines 3 & 4: Solid & broken /

Lines 5 & 6: Solid & broken \

Lesson 8 *Line tracing.* Six lines for writing.

Lines 1 & 2: Solid & broken |

Lines 3 & 4: Solid & broken /

Line 5 & 6: Solid & broken \

Lesson 9 *Line tracing.* Six lines for writing.

Lines 1 & 2: Solid & broken Λ

Lines 3 & 4: Solid & broken V

Line 5: Solid & broken V

Line 6: Solid & broken Λ

Lesson 10 *Practice on template.*

Line 1: / /

Line 2: \ \

Line 3: | |

Line 4: O o

Line 5: Λ Λ

Line 6: V V

Lesson 11 *Half-circle tracing practice.* Trace half circles in pictures.

Lesson 12 *Writing motor skills practice.* Eight lines for writing.

Line 1:

Line 2:

Lines 3 & 4:

Lines 5 & 6:

Line 7:

Line 8:

Lesson 13 *Writing motor skills practice.* Eight lines for writing.

Lines 1 & 2: Solid & broken ∪

Lines 3 & 4: Solid & broken ⋃

Lines 5 & 6: Solid & broken ∩

Lines 7 & 8: Solid & broken ⋂

Lesson 14 Lines 1 & 2: Solid & broken c

Lines 3 & 4: Solid & broken C

Lines 5 & 6: Solid & broken ɔ

Lines 7 & 8: Solid & broken Ɔ

Lesson 15 *Review line and circle tracing* using all the strokes they have learned.

Lesson 16 First 3 letters are solid, rest broken. Second line, two are broken and the rest the child does on his own. Lines 7 & 8 words are for child to trace on Line 7 and write by himself on Line 8.

Lines 1 & 2: a

Lines 3 & 4: o

Lines 5 & 6: d

Lines 7 & 8: do ad add dad

Lesson 17 Lines 1 & 2: c

Lines 3 & 4: e

Lines 5 & 6: c o e a d

Lines 7 & 8: ace odd doe code

Lesson 18 Lines 1 & 2: b

Lines 3 & 4: p

Lines 5 & 6: a b c d e o p

Lines 7 & 8: cab dab pad bad

Lesson 19 Lines 1 & 2: g

Lines 3 & 4: q

Lines 5 & 6: o p q

Lines 7 & 8: go dog pod bag

Lesson 20	Lines 1 & 2:	a b c d e
	Lines 3 & 4:	o p q
	Lines 5 & 6:	go dog pod bag
	Lines 7 & 8:	do odd ace doe
Lesson 21	Lines 1 & 2:	i
	Lines 3 & 4:	l
	Lines 5 & 6:	t
	Lines 7 & 8:	it lit bit pit
Lesson 22	Lines 1 & 2:	n
	Lines 3 & 4:	m
	Lines 5 & 6:	h
	Lines 7 & 8:	mat hat bat pat
Lesson 23	Lines 1 & 2:	r
	Lines 3 & 4:	l m n o p q r
	Lines 5 & 6:	h i
	Lines 7 & 8:	met pet rat art
Lesson 24	Lines 1 & 2:	a b c d e
	Lines 3 & 4:	g h i
	Lines 5 & 6:	it
	Lines 7 & 8:	ham man ran tan
Lesson 25	Line 1:	1
	Line 2:	2
	Line 3:	3
	Line 4:	4
	Line 5:	5
	Line 6:	1 2 3 4 5
Lesson 26	Student begins writing full name.	
	Lines 1 & 2:	v
	Lines 3 & 4:	w
	Lines 5 & 6:	v w v w
	Lines 7 & 8:	we van wet vet
Lesson 27	Lines 1 & 2:	x
	Lines 3 & 4:	z
	Lines 5 & 6:	y
	Lines 7 & 8:	zoo ax x–ray zip

Lesson 28 Lines 1 & 2: u

Lines 3 & 4: s

Lines 5 & 6: v w x y z

Lines 7 & 8: you us so see

Lesson 29 Lines 1 & 2: s t u v w x y z

Lines 3 & 4: yes yet sat set

Line 5: ! ?

Line 6: . ,

Line 7: : ;

Line 8: ! ? . , : ;

Lesson 30 Line 1: 6

Line 2: 7

Line 3: 8

Line 4: 9

Line 5: 0

Line 6: 1 2 3 4 5

Line 7: 6 7 8 9 0

Line 8: Blank line for student to write all numbers.

Lesson 31 Lines 1 & 2: f

Lines 3 & 4: j

Lines 5 & 6: k

Lines 7 & 8: fan fat fit fun

Lesson 32 Lines 1 & 2: a b c d e f g h i

Lines 3 & 4: j k l m n o p q

Lines 5 & 6: r s t u v w x y z

Lines 7 & 8: jam jet jump joy

Lesson 33 Lines 1 & 2: a b c d e f g h i

Lines 3 & 4: j k l m n o p q

Lines 5 & 6: r s t u v w x y z

Lines 7 & 8: kit ask back sock

Lesson 34 Practice words by tracing the letters.

Line 1: do ad add dad

Line 2: ace odd doe code

Line 3: cab dab pad bad

Line 4: go dog pod bag

Line 5: it lit bit pit

Line 6: mat hat bat pat

Line 7: met pet rat art

Line 8: ham man ran tan

Lesson 35 Review and trace all words and numbers in order of appearance.

Line 1: we van wet vet

Line 2: zoo ax x-ray zip

Line 3: you us so see

Line 4: yes yet sat set

Line 5: fan fat fit fun

Line 6: jam jet jump joy

Line 7: kit ask back sock

Line 8: 1 2 3 4 5 6 7 8 9 10

Lesson 36 Lines 1 & 2: O o

Lines 3 & 4: C c

Lines 5 & 6: G g

Lines 7 & 8: God Oh! Come

Lesson 37 Lines 1 & 2: Q q

Lines 3 & 4: J j

Lines 5 & 6: D d

Lines 7 & 8: David Jill Queen

Lesson 38 Lines 1 & 2: P p

Lines 3 & 4: B b

Lines 5 & 6: R r

Lines 7 & 8: Peter Bill Ruth

Lesson 39 Copy verse: God is love. (1 John 4:16)

Lesson 40 Copy verse on special page.

Lesson 41 Lines 1 & 2: V v

Lines 3 & 4: W w

Lines 5 & 6: X x

Lines 7 & 8: Vince Wendy X-ray

Lesson 42 Lines 1 & 2: Y y

Lines 3 & 4: Z z

Lines 5 & 6: A a

Lines 7 & 8: Yes! Zachary Ann

Lesson 43 Lines 1 & 2: M m

Lines 3 & 4: N n

	Lines 5 & 6:	S s
	Lines 7 & 8:	Mary Nancy Sam
Lesson 44	Copy verse:	Love your neighbor as yourself. (Matthew 19:19)
Lesson 45	Copy verse on special page.	
Lesson 46	Lines 1 & 2:	E e
	Lines 3 & 4:	F f
	Lines 5 & 6:	H h
	Lines 7 & 8:	Ellen Frank Holly
Lesson 47	Lines 1 & 2:	T t
	Lines 3 & 4:	I i
	Lines 5 & 6:	L l
	Lines 7 & 8:	Thomas Israel Lord
Lesson 48	Lines 1 & 2:	K k
	Lines 3 & 4:	U u
	Lines 5 & 6:	Kathy Uriah
	Lines 7 & 8:	Keep safe refuge
Lesson 49	Copy verse:	Keep me safe, O God, for in you I take refuge. (Psalm 16:1)
Lesson 50	Copy verse on special page.	
Lesson 51	Practice all capital letters.	
Lesson 52	Practice all lowercase letters.	
Lesson 53	Lines 1 & 2:	Give thanks
	Lines 3 & 4:	to the Lord
	Lines 5 & 6:	for He
	Lines 7 & 8:	is good.
Lesson 54	Copy verse:	Give thanks to the Lord, for he is good. (Psalm 106:1)
Lesson 55	Copy verse on special page.	
Lesson 56	Lines 1 & 2:	A a
	Lines 3 & 4:	B b
	Lines 5 & 6:	M m
	Lines 7 & 8:	Mary saw Ann and Bob.
Lesson 57	Lines 1 & 2:	Blessed
	Lines 3 & 4:	are
	Lines 5 & 6:	the
	Lines 7 & 8:	Blessed be God!
Lesson 58	Lines 1 & 2:	poor
	Lines 3 & 4:	in

	Lines 5 & 6:	Spirit
	Lines 7 & 8:	God loves the poor.
Lesson 59	Copy verse:	Blessed are the poor in spirit. (Matthew 5:3)
Lesson 60	Copy verse on special page.	
Lesson 61	Lines 1 & 2:	C c
	Lines 3 & 4:	L l
	Lines 5 & 6:	J j
	Lines 7 & 8:	The Lord Jesus saves us.
Lesson 62	Lines 1 & 2:	Come
	Lines 3 & 4:	Lord
	Lines 5 – 8:	Jesus comes into our hearts.
Lesson 63	Lines 1 & 2:	R r
	Lines 3 & 4:	Revelation
	Lines 5 & 6:	John wrote the
	Lines 7 & 8:	book of Revelation.
Lesson 64	Copy verse:	Come, Lord Jesus. (Revelation 22:20)
Lesson 65	Copy verse on special page.	
Lesson 66	Lines 1 & 2:	D d
	Lines 3 & 4:	G g
	Lines 5 & 6:	F f
	Lines 7 & 8:	David loves God.
Lesson 67	Lines 1 & 2:	Glory
	Lines 3 & 4:	God
	Lines 5 & 6:	favor
	Lines 7 & 8:	Give God glory!
Lesson 68	Lines 1 & 2:	highest
	Lines 3 & 4:	peace
	Lines 5 & 6:	earth
	Lines 7 & 8:	Pray for peace on earth.
Lesson 69	Copy verse:	Glory to God in the highest, and on earth peace to men on whom His favor rests. (Luke 2:14)
Lesson 70	Copy verse on special page.	
Lesson 71	Lines 1 & 2:	E e
	Lines 3 & 4:	H h
	Lines 5 & 6:	T t
	Lines 7 & 8:	The Lord is near.

Lesson 72	Lines 1 & 2:	shepherds
	Lines 3 & 4:	baby
	Lines 5 & 6:	manger
	Lines 7 & 8:	The shepherds saw the baby Jesus.
Lesson 73	Lines 1 & 2:	Mary
	Lines 3 & 4:	Joseph
	Lines 5 & 6:	found
	Lines 7 & 8:	Mary and Joseph loved Jesus.
Lesson 74	Copy verse:	The shepherds found Mary and Joseph, and the baby, who was lying in a manger. (Luke 2:16)
Lesson 75	Copy verse on special page.	
Lesson 76	Lines 1 & 2:	I i
	Lines 3 & 4:	K k
	Lines 5 & 6:	N n
	Lines 7 & 8:	Isaiah was a prophet.
Lesson 77	Lines 1 & 2:	Arise
	Lines 3 & 4:	shine
	Lines 5 & 6:	light
	Lines 7 & 8:	Jesus is our light.
Lesson 78	Lines 1 & 2:	your
	Lines 3 & 4:	come
	Lines 5 & 6:	Isaiah
	Lines 7 & 8:	Let your light shine.
Lesson 79	Copy verse:	Arise, shine, for your light has come. (Isaiah 60:1)
Lesson 80	Copy verse on special page.	
Lesson 81	Lines 1 & 2:	Aa Bb Cc Dd Ee
	Lines 3 & 4:	Ff Gg Hh Ii Jj
	Lines 5 & 6:	Kk Ll Mm Nn Oo
	Lines 7 & 8:	Pp Qq Rr Ss Tt
Lesson 82	Lines 1 & 2:	Uu Vv Ww Xx
	Lines 3 & 4:	Yy Zz
	Lines 5 & 6:	weary
	Lines 7 & 8:	burdened
Lesson 83	Lines 1 & 2:	Come to me,
	Lines 3 & 4:	all you who are
	Lines 5 & 6:	weary and burdened,
	Lines 7 & 8:	and I will give you rest.

Lesson 84	Copy verse:	Come to me, all you who are weary and burdened, and I will give you rest. (Matthew 11:28)
Lesson 85	Copy verse on special page.	
Lesson 86	Lines 1 & 2:	O o
	Lines 3 & 4:	P p
	Lines 5 & 6:	Q q
	Lines 7 & 8:	I will praise the Lord.
Lesson 87	Lines 1 & 2:	Lord
	Lines 3 & 4:	heart
	Lines 5 & 6:	My heart will
	Lines 7 & 8:	praise the Lord.
Lesson 88	Lines 1 & 2:	Psalm
	Lines 3 & 4:	praise
	Lines 5 & 6:	with all my heart
	Lines 7 & 8:	Psalms praise the Lord.
Lesson 89	Copy verse:	I will praise you, O Lord, with all my heart. (Psalm 138:1)
Lesson 90	Copy verse on special page.	
Lesson 91	Lines 1 & 2:	R r
	Lines 3 & 4:	S s
	Lines 5 & 6:	U u
	Lines 7 & 8:	Blank lines for additional practice.
Lesson 92	Lines 1 & 2:	remember
	Lines 3 & 4:	when
	Lines 5 & 6:	kingdom
	Lines 7 & 8:	Remember me, Jesus.
Lesson 93	Lines 1 & 2:	Luke
	Lines 3 & 4:	Come into my kingdom.
	Lines 5 & 6:	Let me come
	Lines 7 & 8:	into your kingdom.
Lesson 94	Copy verse:	Jesus, remember me when you come into your kingdom. (Luke 23:42)
Lesson 95	Copy verse on special page.	
Lesson 96	Lines 1 & 2:	V v
	Lines 3 & 4:	W w
	Lines 5 & 6:	X x
	Lines 7 & 8:	Blank lines for additional practice.

Lesson 97	Lines 1 & 2:	Father
	Lines 3 & 4:	commend
	Lines 5 & 6:	hands
	Lines 7 & 8:	spirit
Lesson 98	Lines 1 & 2:	Father, into
	Lines 3 & 4:	your hands
	Lines 5 & 6:	I commend
	Lines 7 & 8:	my Spirit.
Lesson 99	Copy verse:	Father, into your hands I commend my Spirit. (Luke 23:46)
Lesson 100	Copy verse on special page.	
Lesson 101	Lines 1 & 2:	Y y
	Lines 3 & 4:	Z z
	Lines 5 & 6:	Matthew 28:5–6
	Lines 7 & 8:	Do not be afraid.
Lesson 102	Lines 1 & 2:	risen
	Lines 3 & 4:	Matthew
	Lines 5 & 6:	know
	Lines 7 & 8:	He is risen.
Lesson 103	Lines 1 & 2:	looking
	Lines 3 & 4:	looking for Jesus
	Lines 5 & 6:	as he said
	Lines 7 & 8:	...He is not here;
Lesson 104	Copy verse:	Do not be afraid, for I know you are looking for Jesus, ... He is not here; he is risen, just as he said. (Matthew 28:5–6)
Lesson 105	Copy verse on special page.	
Lesson 106	Lines 1 & 2:	L l
	Lines 3 & 4:	my light
	Lines 5 & 6:	my salvation
	Lines 7 & 8:	Blank lines for additional practice.
Lesson 107	Lines 1 & 2:	The Lord is my light.
	Lines 3 & 4:	The Lord is my salvation.
	Lines 5 & 6:	Whom shall I fear?
	Lines 7 & 8:	Blank lines for additional practice.
Lesson 108	Lines 1 & 2:	The Lord is my life.
	Lines 3 – 8:	Blank lines for story writing.

Lesson 109	Copy verse:	The Lord is my light and my salvation – whom shall I fear? (Psalm 27:1)
Lesson 110	Copy verse on special page.	
Lesson 111	Lines 1 & 2:	Psalm 100:1–2
	Lines 3 & 4:	Shout
	Lines 5 & 6:	worship
	Lines 7 & 8:	gladness
Lesson 112	Lines 1 & 2:	Shout for joy.
	Lines 3 & 4:	Worship the Lord.
	Lines 5 & 6:	Come before him.
	Lines 7 & 8:	Blank lines for additional practice.
Lesson 113	Lines 1 & 2:	Sing joyful songs.
	Lines 3 & 4:	Sing to the Lord.
	Lines 5 & 6:	Worship with gladness.
	Lines 7 & 8:	Practice semicolon (;)
Lesson 114	Copy verse:	Shout for joy to the Lord, all the earth. Worship the Lord with gladness; come before him with joyful songs. (Psalm 100:1–2)
Lesson 115	Copy verse on special page.	
Lesson 116	Lines 1 & 2:	know
	Lines 3 & 4:	people
	Lines 5 & 6:	pasture
	Lines 7 & 8:	Blank lines for additional practice.
Lesson 117	Lines 1 & 2:	The Lord is God.
	Lines 3 & 4:	He made us.
	Lines 5 & 6:	We are his people.
	Lines 7 & 8:	Blank lines for additional practice.
Lesson 118	Lines 1 & 2:	We are like his sheep.
	Lines 3 & 4:	We rest in his pasture.
	Lines 5 & 6:	He is our shepherd.
	Lines 7 & 8:	Blank lines for additional practice.
Lesson 119	Copy verse:	Know that the Lord is God. It is he who made us, and we are his people, the sheep of his pasture. (Psalm 100:3)
Lesson 120	Copy verse on special page.	
Lesson 121	Lines 1 & 2:	Enter
	Lines 3 & 4:	gates
	Lines 5 & 6:	thanksgiving
	Lines 7 & 8:	Blank lines for additional practice.

Lesson 122	Lines 1 & 2:	courts
	Lines 3 & 4:	praise
	Lines 5 & 6:	Give thanks to him.
	Lines 7 & 8:	Blank lines for additional practice.
Lesson 123	Lines 1 & 2:	Praise his name.
	Lines 3 & 4:	Enter his gates
	Lines 5 & 6:	with thanksgiving.
	Lines 7 & 8:	Blank lines for additional practice.
Lesson 124	Copy verse:	Enter his gates with thanksgiving and his courts with praise; give thanks to him and praise his name. (Psalm 100:4)
Lesson 125	Copy verse on special page.	
Lesson 126	Lines 1 & 2:	endures
	Lines 3 & 4:	forever
	Lines 5 & 6:	faithfulness
	Lines 7 & 8:	Blank lines for additional practice.
Lesson 127	Lines 1 & 2:	continues
	Lines 3 & 4:	generations
	Lines 5 & 6:	through
	Lines 7 & 8:	Blank lines for additional practice.
Lesson 128	Lines 1 & 2:	The Lord is good.
	Lines 3 & 4:	His love endures forever.
	Lines 5 & 6:	He is faithful.
	Lines 7 & 8:	Blank lines for additional practice.
Lesson 129	Copy verse:	For the Lord is good and his love endures forever; his faithfulness continues through all generations. (Psalm 100:5)
Lesson 130	Copy verse on special page.	
Lesson 131	Lines 1 & 2:	Aa Bb Cc Dd Ee
	Lines 3 & 4:	Father
	Lines 5 & 6:	Heaven
	Lines 7 & 8:	Blank lines for additional practice.
Lesson 132	Lines 1 & 2:	hallowed
	Lines 3 & 4:	name
	Lines 5 & 6:	Our Father
	Lines 7 & 8:	Blank lines for additional practice.

Lesson 133 Lines 1 & 2: Father in heaven
Lines 3 & 4: Holy is your name.
Lines 5 & 6: You are our Father.
Lines 7 & 8: Blank lines for additional practice.

Lesson 134 Copy verse: Our Father in heaven, hallowed be your name. (Matthew 6:9)

Lesson 135 Copy verse on special page.

Lesson 136 Lines 1 & 2: Ff Gg Hh Ii Jj
Lines 3 & 4: kingdom
Lines 5 & 6: will
Lines 7 & 8: Blank lines for additional practice.

Lesson 137 Lines 1 & 2: earth
Lines 3 & 4: Your kingdom come.
Lines 5 & 6: Your will be done.
Lines 7 & 8: Blank lines for additional practice.

Lesson 138 Lines 1 & 2: on earth
Lines 3 & 4: as it is in heaven
Lines 5 & 6: Blank lines for additional practice.
Lines 7 & 8: Blank lines for additional practice.

Lesson 139 Copy verse: Your kingdom come, your will be done on earth as it is in heaven. (Matthew 6:10)

Lesson 140 Copy verse on special page.

Lesson 141 Lines 1 & 2: Kk Ll Mm Nn Oo
Lines 3 & 4: Give
Lines 5 & 6: bread
Lines 7 & 8: Blank lines for additional practice.

Lesson 142 Lines 1 & 2: daily
Lines 3 & 4: Give God praise.
Lines 5 & 6: Give us our daily bread.
Lines 7 & 8: Blank lines for additional practice.

Lesson 143 Lines 1 & 2: Give us today
Lines 3 & 4: your blessing.
Lines 5 & 6: Blank lines for additional practice.
Lines 7 & 8: Blank lines for additional practice.

Lesson 144 Copy verse: Give us today our daily bread. (Matthew 6:11)

Lesson 145 Copy verse on special page.

Lesson 146 Lines 1 & 2: Pp Qq Rr Ss Tt
Lines 3 & 4: Forgive
Lines 5 & 6: debts
Lines 7 & 8: Blank lines for additional practice.

Lesson 147 Lines 1 & 2: forgiven
Lines 3 & 4: debtors
Lines 5 & 6: Forgive us.
Lines 7 & 8: Lines 1 & 2:

Lesson 148 Lines 1 & 2: We forgive.
Lines 3 & 4: Father forgive.
Lines 5 & 6: Forgive us as we
Lines 7 & 8: also have forgiven.

Lesson 149 Copy verse: Forgive us our debts, as we also have forgiven our debtors. (Matthew 6:12)

Lesson 150 Copy verse on special page.

Lesson 151 Lines 1 & 2: Uu Vv Ww Xx Yy Zz
Lines 3 & 4: lead
Lines 5 & 6: temptation
Lines 7 & 8: Blank lines for additional practice.

Lesson 152 Lines 1 & 2: deliver
Lines 3 & 4: evil
Lines 5 & 6: Deliver us from evil.
Lines 7 & 8: Blank lines for additional practice.

Lesson 153 Lines 1 & 2: Lead us away from evil.
Lines 3 & 4: Lead us not
Lines 5 & 6: into temptation.
Lines 7 & 8: Blank lines for additional practice.

Lesson 154 Copy verse: And lead us not into temptation, but deliver us from the evil one. (Matthew 6:13)

Lesson 155 Copy verse on special page.

Lesson 156 Practice all capital letters.

Lesson 157 Practice all lowercase letters and numbers.

Lesson 158 Practice writing favorite verse.

Lesson 159 Practice writing own sentences.

Lesson 160 Copy the Lord's Prayer on three special pages.

Teacher Lessons

Lesson 1 - Circle Practice

Teaching Tips:

Although the children will not be writing a Bible verse as part of the weekly lesson for the first seven weeks, begin now to prepare them for that time. Select a verse for the week, either the suggested one given or another that may fit with your lessons. Write the verse out in manuscript on the chalkboard or a piece of poster board so that the children can see it while they do their work. Use it as a prayer throughout the week. Talk about it. Read it in context.

1. Introduce the lesson by telling the children that many letters are made up of circles or parts of circles. Have the children locate circular shapes in the room, outdoors, at home, or wherever they are.
2. Do some warm-up activities. Have the children practice making circles with their fingers in the air, on the wall or floor, on the desk or table with their fingers, on the palm of their hand, or on each other's backs. Give opportunities throughout the week for the children to paint circles, draw them on the board, or to use other tactile materials (sand, clay, etc.) to form circles.
3. Talk about the picture in Lesson 1. Josh and Julie, with pencils in hand, are dancing in space ready to capture and trace all the circles in the picture.
4. Have the children take their pencils. Check their sitting position and the position of paper and pencil. This can be done initially as a game or drill if you have the students pretend they are astronauts like Josh and Julie and are going through a checklist to make sure things are "A-OK" before blast-off:

Teacher:	"Sitting up tall?"
Students:	"Check."
Teacher:	"Paper slanted?"
Students:	"Check."
Teacher:	"Pencil position?"
Students:	"Check."
Teacher:	"Hand positions?"
Students:	"Check."

5. Check each student's position to see if he/she is ready to write.
6. Have the children write their first name on the top line.
7. Have the children trace each circle in the picture. Urge them to do it with care.
8. Check work and positions.
9. Children may color the picture when finished.

Suggested Bible Verse Lessons 1-5:

"Whatever you do, work at it with all your heart, as working for the Lord, not for men." (Colossians 3:23)

Lesson 2 - Circle Practice

Teaching Tips:

1. Do some warm-up activities. Have the children practice making circles in the air, on the wall or floor, on the desk or table with their fingers, on the palm of their hand, or on each other's backs. Give opportunities throughout the week for the children to paint circles, draw them on the board, or to use other tactile materials (sand, clay, etc.) to form circles.
2. Talk about the picture in Lesson 2. Let the students use their imaginations to describe the picture.
3. Have the children take their pencils. Check their sitting position and the position of paper and pencil. This can be done initially as a game or drill if you explain to the students that the following is a checklist similar to a pre-flight checklist astronauts have to make sure things are OK before blast-off:

Teacher:	"Sitting up tall?"
Students:	"Check."
Teacher:	"Paper slanted?"
Students:	"Check."
Teacher:	"Pencil position?"
Students:	"Check."
Teacher:	"Hand positions?"
Students:	"Check."

4. Check each student's position to see if he/she is ready to write.
5. Have the children write their first name on the top line.
6. Have the children trace each circle in the picture. Urge them to do it with care.

7. Check work and positions.
8. Children may color the picture when finished.

Suggested Bible Verse Lessons 1-5:

"Whatever you do, work at it with all your heart, as working for the Lord, not for men."
(Colossians 3:23)

Lesson 3 - Manuscript Circle Practice

Teaching Tips:

1. In this lesson, the children begin practicing manuscript circles (the letter **Oo**). Using an alphabet chart, have the children find all of the letters which use a circle or part of a circle in the formation of the letter.
2. Tell the children that circles in manuscript writing have a special starting point.
3. Use a clock to demonstrate the "two o'clock" position. This can be done on a real clock face or on one drawn on the board or an a chart.
4. Have the children do their warm-up exercises, making sure that they begin their circles in the two o'clock position and proceed up, over, and around (counterclockwise).
5. Look at today's lesson page. Tell the children that the rocket ship will be their guide for forming letters in these early lessons. The rocket ship has a nose cone, a second stage, a booster, and a tail. Ask them what parts of the rocket the large circle covers (second stage and booster). What part of the rocket does the small circle cover? (only the booster)
6. Have the children write their first name on the top line.
7. Review with them the idea that everything they do is to be done carefully to praise God. They are not to rush through the tracing of the circles, but to do each one the best they can.

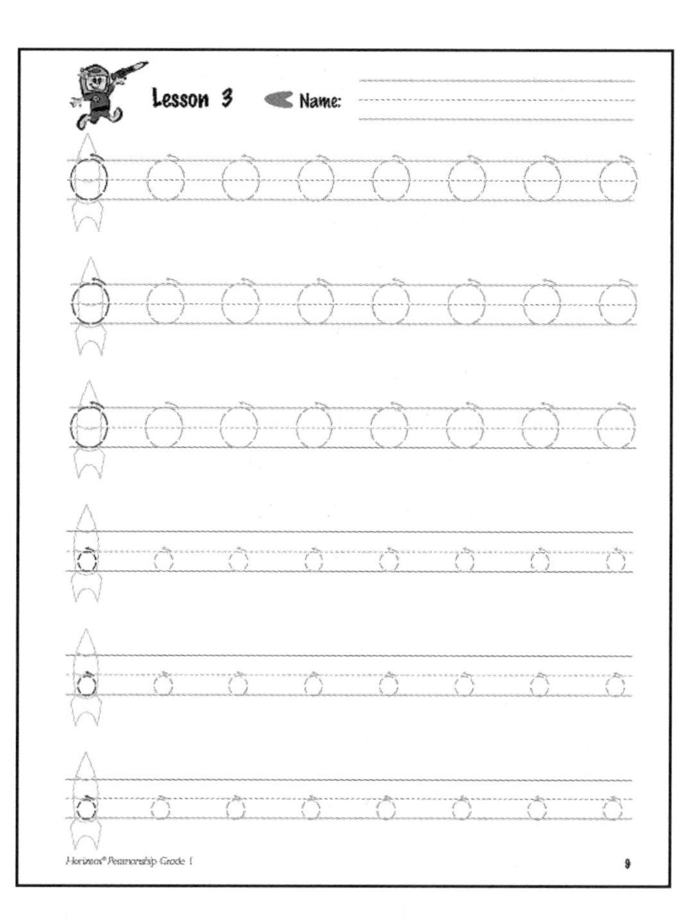

8. Do the position checklist. Monitor the children as they practice. Compliment careful efforts.
9. Take a break after the first three lines. Have the children stand, shake their hands and arms, and trace some circles in the air.
10. Proceed with the small circles.
11. Praise all efforts. Circle the best on the page as a model.

Suggested Bible Verse Lessons 1-5:

"Whatever you do, work at it with all your heart, as working for the Lord, not for men." (Colossians 3:23)

Lesson 4 - Circle Practice

Teaching Tips:

1. Do warm-up activities.
2. Introduce the page.
3. Instruct the children to use the empty box on the page to create their own "circle" pictures. Talk about what they might include in their pictures.
4. When they have finished the picture, they will trace the two lines of circles at the bottom of the page.
5. Have the children do their own position checks, but observe their position and correct as needed.

Suggested Bible Verse Lessons 1-5:

"Whatever you do, work at it with all your heart, as working for the Lord, not for men."
(Colossians 3:23)

Lesson 5 - Special Page

Teaching Tips:

1. Do warm-up activities.
2. On this page the children will not only trace the large and small circles but will have the opportunity to show their best circles. This is a special page that they can take home or display as their best work.
3. Have the children take their time. Emphasize the spacing needed between letters (see introductory pages). Have them model the spacing used at the beginning of each line.
4. Encourage the children to stop if their hands become tired and rest for a minute.
5. Allow them to further decorate the page if they choose.

Lesson 6 - Line Practice

Teaching Tips:

1. Have the children practice straight and slanted lines in their warm-up activities.
2. Have them find examples of things with straight lines and slanted lines in their surroundings.
3. Introduce the picture. Have the children find the dotted lines they are to trace.
4. Check writing positions.
5. Trace lines and color picture.

Suggested Bible Verse Lessons 6-10:

"Let everything that has breath praise the Lord." (Psalm 150:6) Continue the emphasis on all things being done for the glory of God.

Lesson 7 - Line Practice

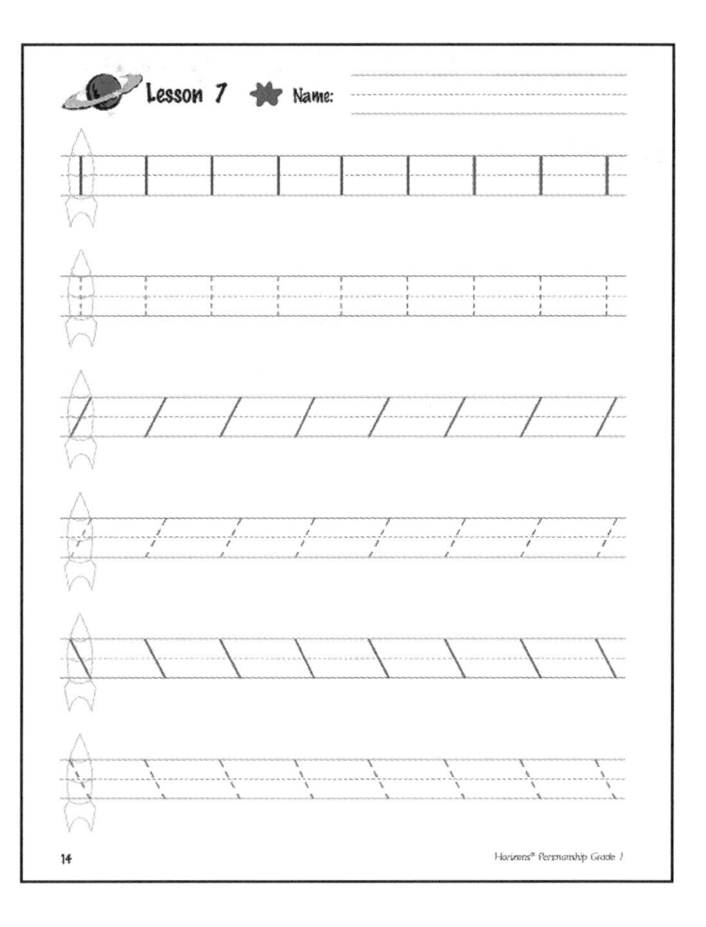

Teaching Tips:

1. Do warm-up activity with both lines and circles.
2. Have the children look at the alphabet chart and find all the letters that use straight lines as part of the letter formation.
3. Have them find all letters that use slanted lines in the formation.
4. Introduce the page. Have the children observe the three types of lines they will practice. What parts of the rocket will be involved? (second stage and booster)
5. Do position check.
6. Observe children at work. Correct position. Compliment all efforts.
7. Break the activity as needed so that the children do not become tired and simply rush through it.

Lesson 8 - Line Practice

Teaching Tips:

1. Warm-up activities and position check.
2. Observe half-line practice (booster only).
3. Proceed as in previous lessons.
4. Remind the children to write their first name on the top line.

Suggested Bible Verse Lessons 6-10:

"Let everything that has breath praise the Lord." (Psalm 150:6) Continue the emphasis on all things being done for the glory of God.

Lesson 9 - Line Practice

Teaching Tips:

1. Warm-up activities and position check.
2. Note the slant of the lines.
3. Note the small diagonal lines. Have the children find the small "v" on the alphabet chart.

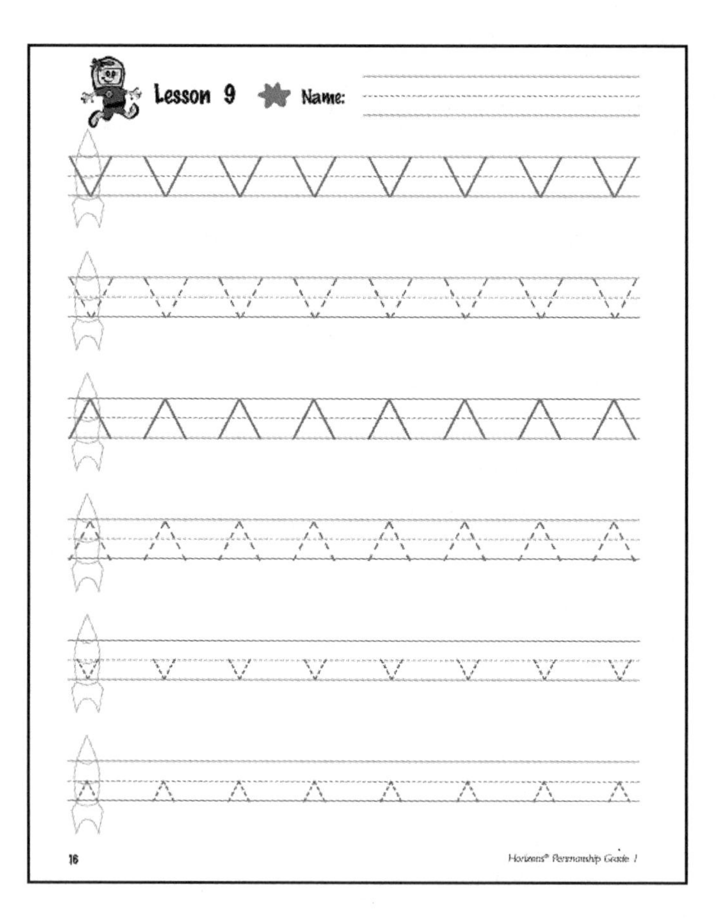

Lesson 10 - Special Page

Teaching Tips:

1. Warm-up activities and position check.
2. Children will finish lines with their own work: check spacing and slant.
3. Children may decorate page when finished.
4. Remind the children to write their first name on the top line.

Suggested Bible Verse Lessons 6-10:

"Let everything that has breath praise the Lord." (Psalm 150:6) Continue the emphasis on all things being done for the glory of God.

Lesson 10 Name:

Horizons® Penmanship Grade 1 17

Lesson 11 - Half-Circle & Stroke Practice

Teaching Tips:

1. Proceed as with circles and lines. Have children think of half-circle objects.
2. Warm-up activities and position check.
3. Picture: find all dotted shapes to trace.
4. Trace objects and color picture when finished. The children may wish to add more half-circle pictures of their own.

Suggested Bible Verse Lessons 11-15:

"But the fruit of the Spirit is love, joy, peace, patience, kindness, goodness, faithfulness, gentleness and self-control."
(Galatians 5:22)

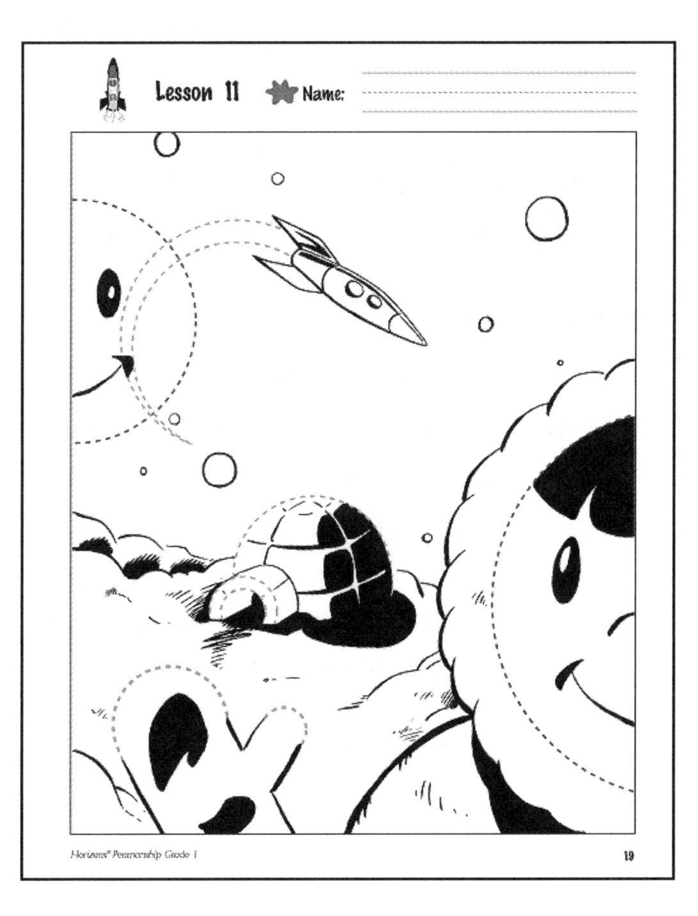

Lesson 12 - Writing Motor Skills Practice

Teaching Tips:

1. Warm-up and position check.
2. Emphasize tracing carefully and slowly.
3. Break as needed.
4. Children requiring additional practice may use the writing motor skills practice pages duplicated from the masters located in the back of the *Teacher's Guide*.
5. Remind the children to write their first name on the top line.

Suggested Bible Verse Lessons 11-15:

"But the fruit of the Spirit is love, joy, peace, patience, kindness, goodness, faithfulness, gentleness and self-control."
(Galatians 5:22)

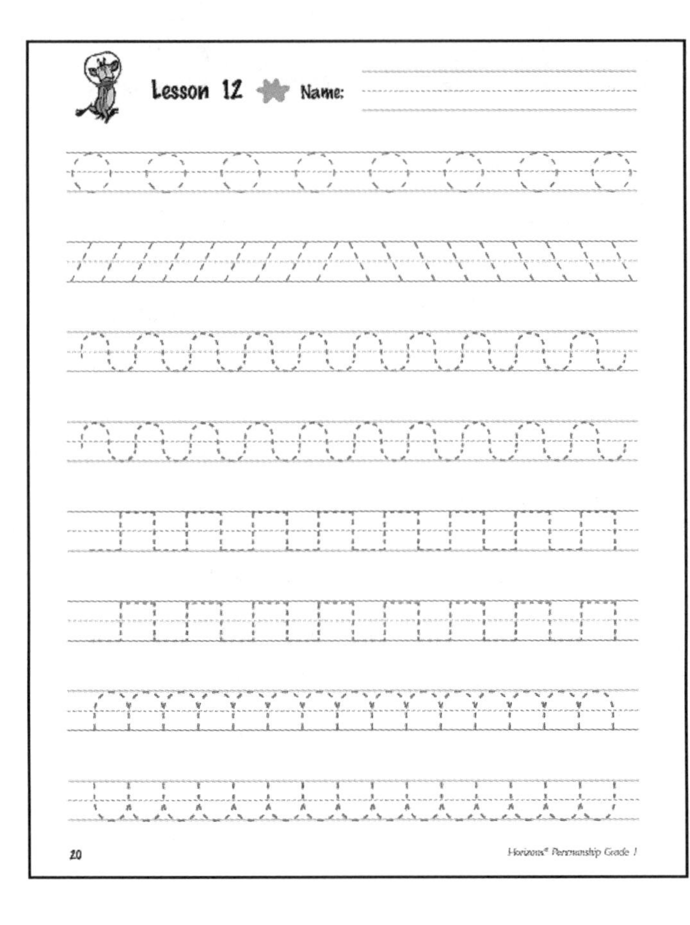

Lesson 13 - Writing Motor Skills Practice

Teaching Tips:

1. Warm-up and position check.
2. Emphasize tracing carefully and slowly.
3. Break as needed.
4. Children requiring additional practice may use the writing motor skills practice pages duplicated from the masters located in the back of the *Teacher's Guide*.

Lesson 14 - Writing Motor Skills Practice

Teaching Tips:

1. Warm-up and position check.
2. Note starting position for the first four lines (two o'clock).
3. Have children identify letters formed in the first four lines (**Cc**).
4. Complete page as in previous lessons.
5. Children requiring additional practice may use the writing motor skills practice pages duplicated from the masters located in the back of the *Teacher's Guide*.

Suggested Bible Verse Lessons 11-15:

"But the fruit of the Spirit is love, joy, peace, patience, kindness, goodness, faithfulness, gentleness and self-control."

(Galatians 5:22)

Lesson 14 Name:

11 Horizons® Penmanship Grade 1

Lesson 15 - Special Page

Teaching Tips:

1. Warm-up and position check.
2. Proceed as in other special pages, observing spacing and slant.
3. Color or decorate page as desired.
4. Remind the children to write their first name on the top line.

Lesson 15 Name:

Horizons® Penmanship Grade 1 23

Lesson 16 - Letters a, o, d

Teaching Tips:

Describe the formation of each letter as it is written, noting its slant, position, and size within the guidelines. Descriptions are given in the lessons and are meant to accompany the demonstration of the letter, not to be used in isolation.

Have the children practice writing the letter in the air, on their hands, on the board, etc.

1. Three letters are introduced in this lesson: **a, o,** and **d**.
2. Have the children identify these letters, find them on the alphabet chart, in names, and on any signs which appear in their immediate surroundings.
3. Talk about the name and the sound each letter makes. Note how each letter is formed (use the rocket reference points):

   a: circle (beginning at two o'clock position), and half-line. Children DO NOT pick up their pencils to make the half-line, but make the circle, then continue up to the dotted tine and down again.

   o: small circle

   d: three-quarter circle (looks like a small "c") and a tall line (up to the top of the second stage). Use a continuous stroke around, up to the top, then down.
4. Go over the four words to be practiced at the bottom of the page. Explain the difference in meaning for "ad" and "add."
5. Warm-up for each letter and check position.

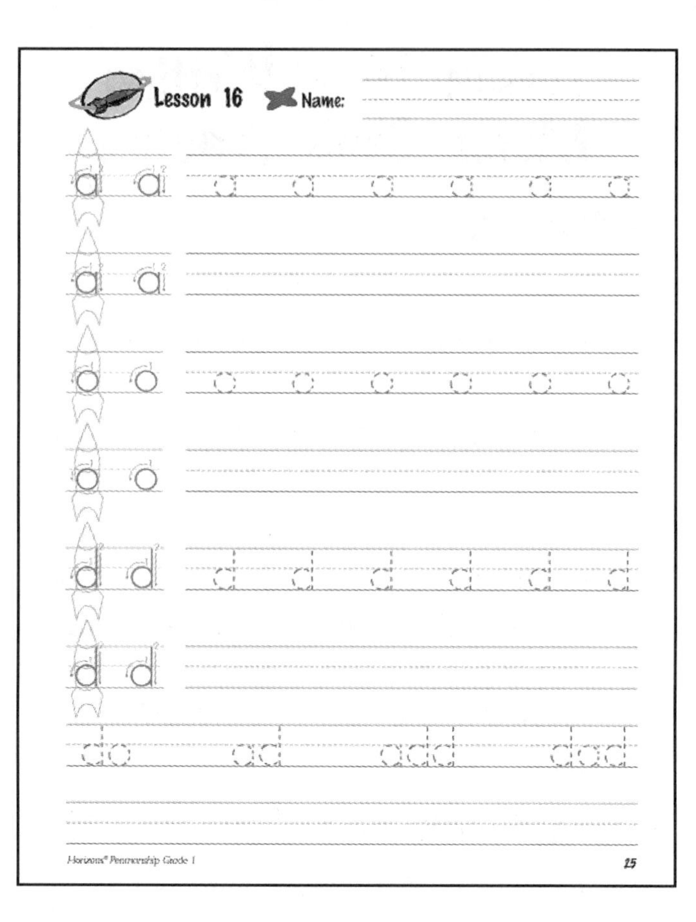

6. Practice the letters. Observe position, formation, and spacing.
7. Praise all efforts.
8. Circle the best attempt for each letter and word.

Suggested Bible Verse Lessons 16-20:

"I will praise you, O Lord, with all my heart; I will tell of all your wonders." (Psalm 9:1)

Lesson 17 - Letters c & e

Teaching Tips:

1. Letters **c** and **e** – Have the children identify these letters, find them on the alphabet chart, in names, and on any signs which appear in their immediate surroundings.
2. Have the children identify these letters, find them on the alphabet chart, in names, and on any signs which appear in their immediate surroundings.
3. Talk about the name and the sound each letter makes. Note how each letter is formed (use the rocket reference points):

   c: as practiced in Lesson 14.

   e: straight line, small **c**. Begin in the middle of the space between the dotted line and the bottom line. Go across and then up and around.
4. Warm-up for each letter and check position.
5. Remind the children to write their first name on the top line.
6. Observe position, formation, and spacing.
7. Letter practice in line 6: trace the letter, then copy it. In line 7 write each letter twice as in line 6.
8. Introduce words for writing practice. Ask the children to find more words using the letters they have learned so far. Trace words and observe spacing.
9. Praise all efforts.
10. Circle the best attempt for each letter and word.

Lesson 17 Name:

26 Horizons® Penmanship Grade 1

Suggested Bible Verse Lessons 16-20:

"I will praise you, O Lord, with all my heart; I will tell of all your wonders." (Psalm 9:1)

Lesson 18 - Letters b & p

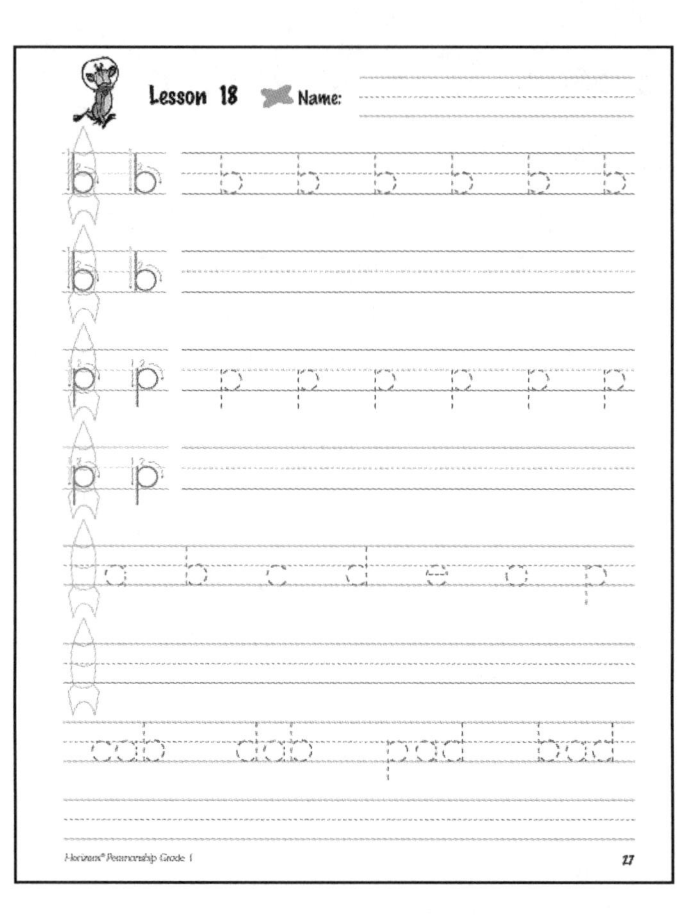

Teaching Tips:

1. Letters **b**, **p** – Note that these letters both begin with lines.
2. Have the children identify these letters, find them on the alphabet chart, in names, and on any signs which appear in their immediate surroundings. Talk about the name and the sound each letter makes. Note how each letter is formed (use the rocket reference points):

   b: tall line (second stage and booster) and circle. One stroke: down, up and around.

   p: line beginning at the dotted line and going down through the booster to the tip of the tail. One stroke: down, up, and around.
3. Warm-up for each letter and check position.
4. Practice the letters. Observe position, formation, and spacing. Watch for letter reversals.
5. Practice lines. See if children notice that the "a, b, c, d, e" are in sequence.
6. Trace letters in line 6. Copy them in line 7.
7. Introduce words, trace and copy. Watch for reversals in the final line.
8. Praise all efforts.
9. Circle the best attempt for each letter and word.

Suggested Bible Verse Lessons 16-20:

"I will praise you, O Lord, with all my heart; I will tell of all your wonders." (Psalm 9:1)

Lesson 19 - Letters g & q

Teaching Tips:

1. Letters **g**, **q** – Note that both letters have a hook on the bottom.
2. Have the children identify these letters, find them on the alphabet chart, in names, and on any signs which appear in their immediate surroundings. Talk about the name and the sound(s) each letter makes. Note how each letter is formed (use the rocket reference points):

   g: small circle and hook. One stroke: around, up, down to the rocket tail, curve back up toward the booster (left side).

   q: small circle and hook. One stroke: around, up, down to the rocket tail, curve away from the rocket. Note that the curve on this letter does not go up as high as the curve on the "g."
3. Warm-up for each letter and check position.
4. Practice the letters. Observe position, formation, and spacing.
5. Practice lines. See if the children recognize that "o, p, q" are in sequence.
6. Trace letters in line 6. Copy them in Line 7.
7. Introduce words, trace and copy.
8. Praise all efforts.
9. Circle the best attempt for each letter and word.

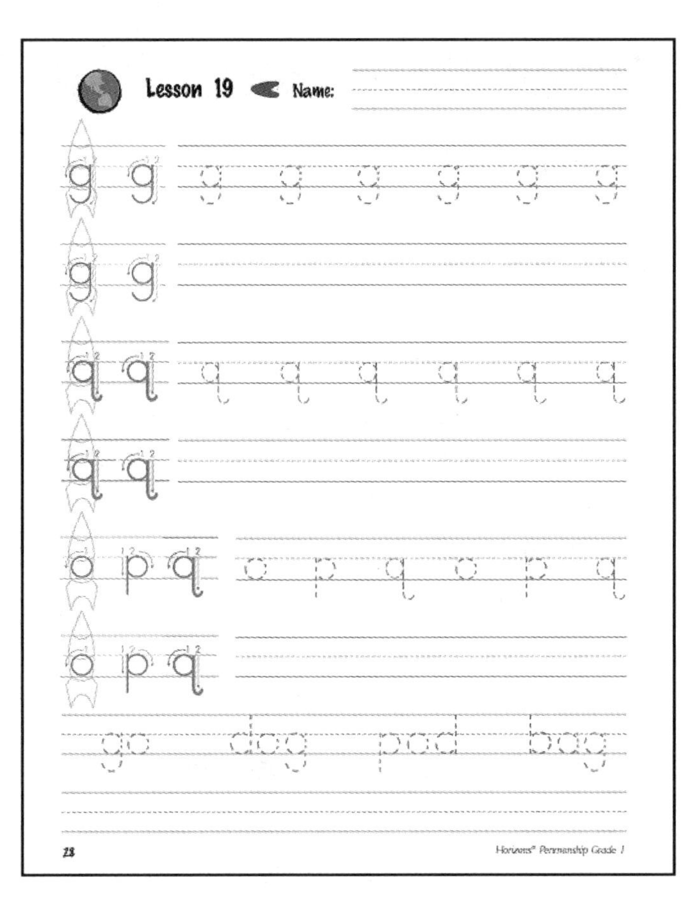

Suggested Bible Verse Lessons 16-20:

"I will praise you, O Lord, with all my heart; I will tell of all your wonders." (Psalm 9:1)

Lesson 20 - Special Page

Teaching Tips:

1. Review the letters and words with the children.
2. Remind the children to write their first name on the top line.
3. Have the children begin writing. This page is designed to show the children's best work for the week.
4. Observe position, formation, and spacing. Watch for reversals.
5. Praise all efforts.
6. Children may decorate the page.

Suggested Bible Verse Lessons 16-20:

"I will praise you, O Lord, with all my heart; I will tell of all your wonders." (Psalm 9:1)

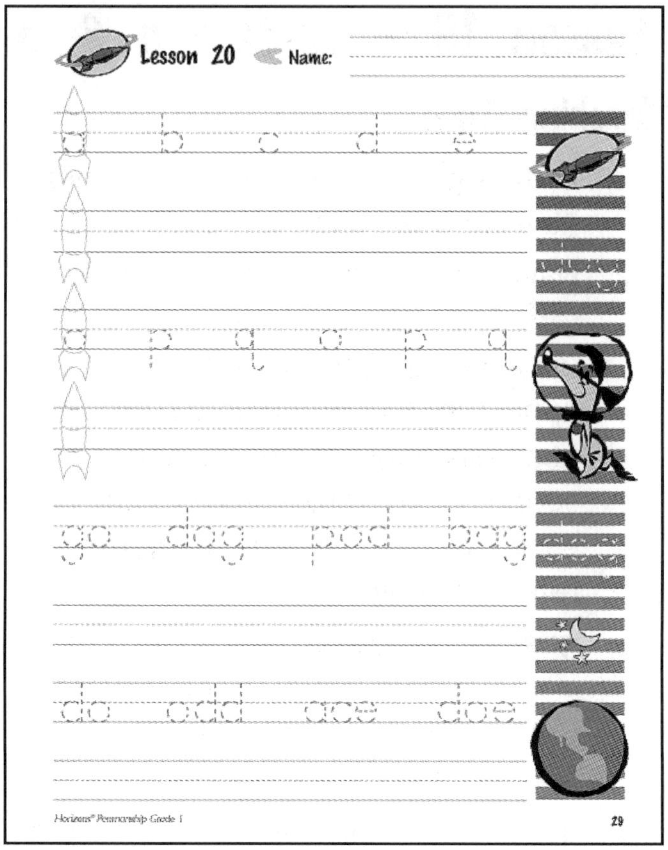

Lesson 21 - Letters i, l, t

Teaching Tips:

1. Letters: **i**, **l**, **t** – Note that we will use three different lengths of lines.
2. **i**: half line and dot. Two strokes needed. Begin the first stroke on the dotted line, down through the booster stage. The second stroke is the dot in the middle of the second stage, just above the line.
3. **l**: One stroke from the top of the second stage to the bottom of the booster stage.
4. **t**: Two strokes are needed: a line beginning in the middle of the second stage and going down to the bottom of the booster and a small line crossing it at the dotted line.
5. Note that all words here rhyme.

Suggested Bible Verse Lessons 21-25:

"O Lord, you have searched me and you know me. You know when I sit and when I rise; you perceive my thoughts from afar."
(Psalm 139:1-2)

NOTE: In all the following lessons, the steps established in the first four weeks should be continued:

1. Have the children identify new letters, find them on the alphabet chart, in names, and on any signs which appear in the room or in their immediate surroundings.
2. Talk about the name and the sound each letter makes. Note how each letter is formed (use the rocket reference points).

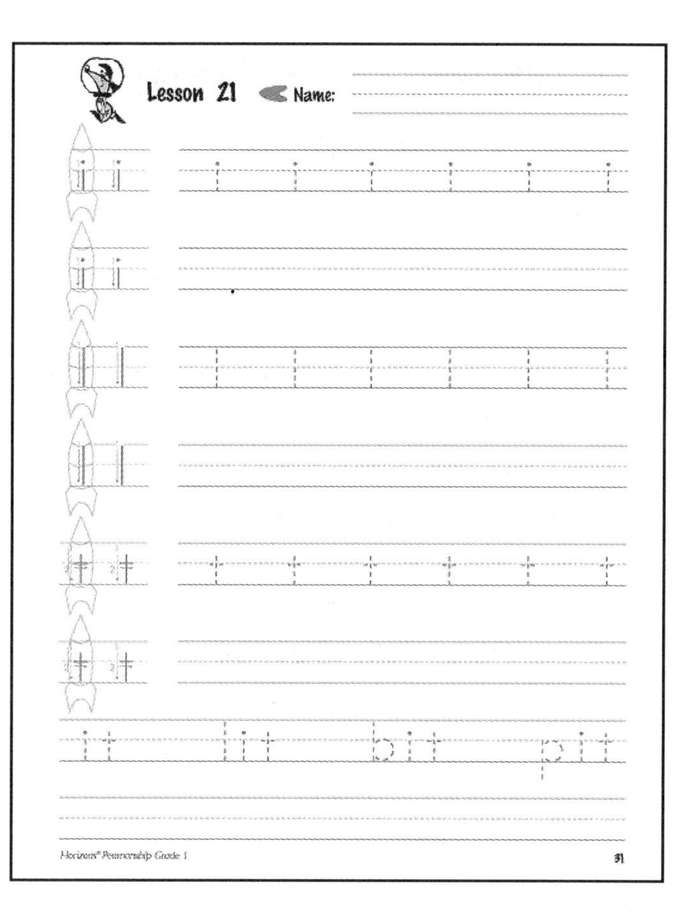

3. Warm-up for each letter and check position.
4. Remind the children to write their first name on the top line.
5. Have the students trace and copy the letters while observing the position, formation, and spacing.
6. Give the children time to rest if needed.
7. Introduce practice lines, sequences of letters, new words. As the children progress in both their writing and reading/phonics skills, they will be able to add more words that rhyme with those given. Encourage their efforts. Move toward writing sentences and stories.
8. Praise all efforts.
9. Circle the best attempt for each letter and word.

Lesson 22 - Letters n, m, h

Teaching Tips:

1. Letters: **n**, **m**, **h** – Note that all three letters have an arched section.
2. **n**: One stroke – half-line and arch filling the booster of the rocket: down, up, around, and down.
3. **m**: One stroke – half-line and two arches filling the booster of the rocket: down, up, around, down, up, around and down again.
4. **h**: One stroke – tall line (second stage and booster) and arch: down, up, around and down.
5. Note that all words here rhyme.
6. Have the children identify new letters, find them on the alphabet chart, in names, and on any signs which appear in the room or in their immediate surroundings.
7. Talk about the name and the sound each letter makes. Note how each letter is formed (use the rocket reference points).
8. Warm-up for each letter and check position.
9. Remind the children to write their first name on the top line.
10. Have the students trace and copy the letters while observing the position, formation, and spacing.
11. Give the children time to rest if needed.
12. Introduce practice lines, sequences of letters, new words. As the children progress in both their writing and reading/phonics skills, they will be able to add more words that rhyme with those given. Encourage their efforts. Move toward writing sentences and stories.
13. Praise all efforts.
14. Circle the best attempt for each letter and word.

Lesson 22 Name:

n n n n n n n n

n n

m m m m m m m m

m m

h h h h h h h h

h h

mat hat bat pat

32 Horizons® Penmanship Grade 1

Suggested Bible Verse Lessons 21-25:

"O Lord, you have searched me and you know me. You know when I sit and when I rise; you perceive my thoughts from afar."

(Psalm 139:1-2)

Lesson 23 - Letter r

Teaching Tips:

1. Letter **r**, review of **l, m, n, o, p, q, r** (sequence)
2. **r**: One stroke – half-line and small curve: down, up, and just around (to about the one o'clock position).
3. Sequence review.
4. Have the children identify the letters, find them on the alphabet chart, in names, and on any signs which appear in the room or in their immediate surroundings.
5. Talk about the name and the sound each letter makes. Note how each letter is formed (use the rocket reference points).
6. Warm-up for each letter and check position.
7. Remind the children to write their first name on the top line.
8. Have the students trace and copy the letters while observing the position, formation, and spacing.
9. Give the children time to rest if needed.
10. Introduce practice lines, sequences of letters, new words. As the children progress in both their writing and reading/phonics skills, they will be able to add more words that rhyme with those given. Encourage their efforts. Move toward writing sentences and stories.
11. Praise all efforts.
12. Circle the best attempt for each letter and word.

Lesson 23 Name:

r r r r r r r r

r r

l m n o p q r

h i h i h i h i h i h i

h i

met pet rat art

Horizons® Penmanship Grade 1 33

Suggested Bible Verse Lessons 21-25:

"O Lord, you have searched me and you know me. You know when I sit and when I rise; you perceive my thoughts from afar."
(Psalm 139:1-2)

Lesson 24 - Review

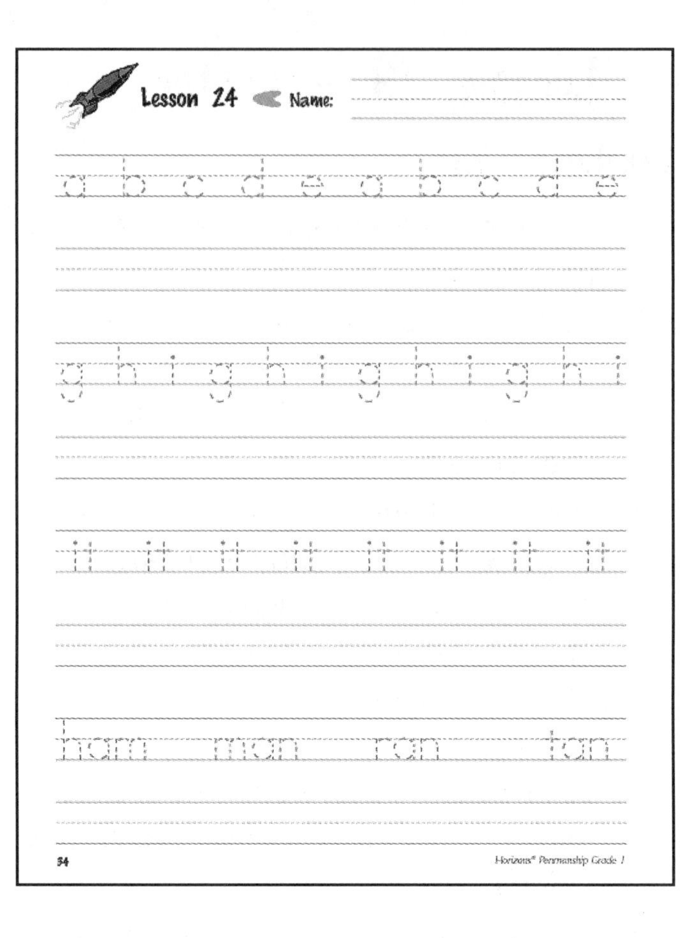

Teaching Tips:

1. Review lesson: **a**, **b**, **c**, **d**, **e**, **g**, **h**, **i**.
2. Watch formation and spacing throughout.
3. Have the children identify the letters, find them on the alphabet chart, in names, and on any signs which appear in the room or in their immediate surroundings.
4. Talk about the name and the sound each letter makes. Note how each letter is formed (use the rocket reference points).
5. Warm-up for each letter and check position.
6. Remind the children to write their first name on the top line.
7. Have the students trace and copy the letters while observing the position, formation, and spacing.
8. Give the children time to rest if needed.
9. Introduce practice lines, sequences of letters, new words. As the children progress in both their writing and reading/phonics skills, they will be able to add more words that rhyme with those given. Encourage their efforts. Move toward writing sentences and stories.
10. Praise all efforts.
11. Circle the best attempt for each letter and word.

Suggested Bible Verse Lessons 21-25:

"O Lord, you have searched me and you know me. You know when I sit and when I rise; you perceive my thoughts from afar."
(Psalm 139:1-2)

Lesson 25 - Number Practice, Special Page

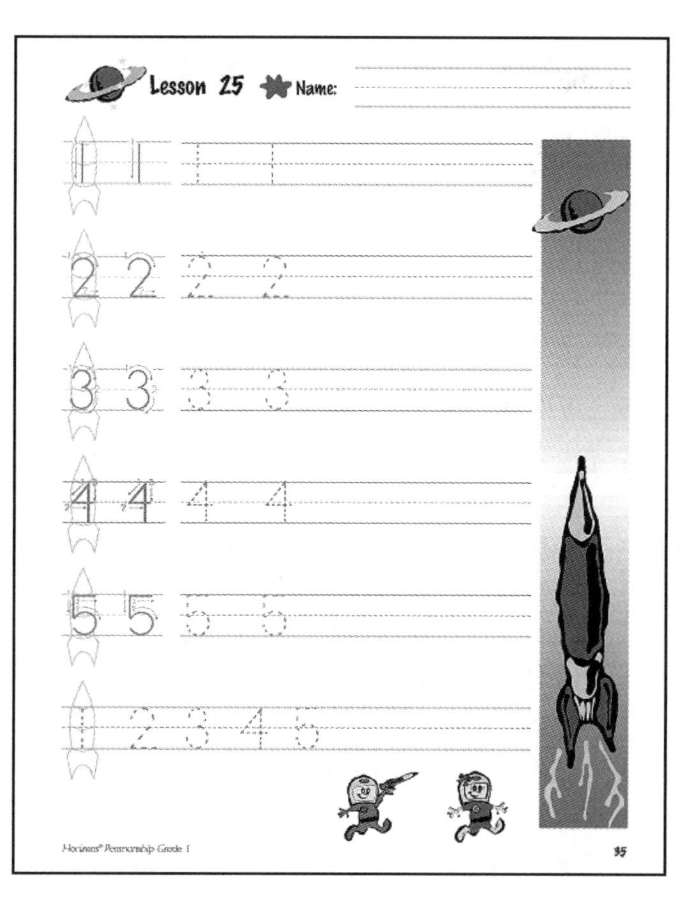

Teaching Tips:

1. Number practice: **1**, **2**, **3**, **4**, **5**. Determine children's knowledge of numbers.
2. **1**: tall line, second stage and booster.
3. **2**: around, down to the bottom line, and across. Begin about the 11 o'clock position.
4. **3**: around and around. Begin about the 11 o'clock position and end at the 8 o'clock position.
5. **4**: two strokes – a slanted line down and across, tall line down.
6. **5**: two strokes – down and around, across the top.
7. Warm-up and check position.
8. Remind the children to write their first name on the top line.
9. Have the students trace and copy the numbers while observing the position, formation, and spacing.
10. Give the children time to rest if needed.
11. Praise all efforts.
12. Circle the best attempt for each number.

Suggested Bible Verse Lessons 21-25:

"O Lord, you have searched me and you know me. You know when I sit and when I rise; you perceive my thoughts from afar."
(Psalm 139:1-2)

Lesson 26 - Letters v, w

Teaching Tips:

1. **v**: One stroke – begin at the dotted line and slant right to bottom, slant back up to dotted line.
2. **w**: One stroke – begin at the dotted line and slant right to bottom, slant back up to dotted line, slant right to bottom, slant back up to dotted line.
3. Have the children identify new letters, find them on the alphabet chart, in names, and on any signs which appear in the room or in their immediate surroundings.
4. Talk about the name and the sound each letter makes. Note how each letter is formed (use the rocket reference points).
5. Warm-up for each letter and check position.
6. Have the children write their FIRST AND LAST NAME on the blank. If they have a long name that will not fit, have them write the first initial and last name. This can also be practiced on a reproducible practice page.
7. Have the students trace and copy the letters while observing the position, formation, and spacing.
8. Give the children time to rest if needed.
9. Introduce practice lines, sequences of letters, new words. As the children progress in both their writing and reading/phonics skills, they will be able to add more words that rhyme with those given. Encourage their efforts. Move toward writing sentences and stories.

Lesson 26 Name:

v v v v v v v v

v v

w w w w w w w w

w w

v w v w v w v w

v w

we van wet vet

Horizons Penmanship Grade 1 37

10. Praise all efforts.
11. Circle the best attempt for each letter and word.

Suggested Bible Verse Lessons 26-30:

"Who can ascend the hill of the Lord? Who may stand in his holy place?"
(Psalm 24:3)

Lesson 27 - Letters
x, y, z

Teaching Tips:

1. **x**: two slanted strokes, each beginning at the dotted line and crossing in the middle of the booster stage.
2. **y**: two slanted strokes, each beginning at the dotted line, the first stopping at the bottom line (booster stage only), the second extending down into the tail.
3. **z**: one stroke covering the booster: across the dotted line, slant line back down to the bottom line, across the bottom.
4. Have the children identify new letters, find them on the alphabet chart, in names, and on any signs which appear in the room or in their immediate surroundings.
5. Talk about the name and the sound each letter makes. Note how each letter is formed (use the rocket reference points).
6. Warm-up for each letter and check position.
7. Remind the children to write both their first and last names on the top line.
8. Have the students trace and copy the letters while observing the position, formation, and spacing.
9. Give the children time to rest if needed.
10. Introduce practice lines, sequences of letters, new words. As the children progress in both their writing and reading/phonics skills, they will be able to add more words that rhyme with those given. Encourage their efforts. Move toward writing sentences and stories.
11. Praise all efforts.
12. Circle the best attempt for each letter and word.

Suggested Bible Verse Lessons 26-30:

"Who can ascend the hill of the Lord? Who may stand in his holy place?"
(Psalm 24:3)

Lesson 28 - Letters u, s

Teaching Tips:

1. **u**: one stroke down, around, up and down.
2. **s**: one stroke that curves its way through the booster: start at the dotted line up and around, down and around the bottom line.
3. Sequence review: **v, w, x, y, z**.
4. Have the children identify new letters, find them on the alphabet chart, in names, and on any signs which appear in the room or in their immediate surroundings.
5. Talk about the name and the sound each letter makes. Note how each letter is formed (use the rocket reference points).
6. Warm-up for each letter and check position.
7. Remind the children to write both their first and last names on the top line.
8. Have the students trace and copy the letters while observing the position, formation, and spacing.
9. Give the children time to rest if needed.
10. Introduce practice lines, sequences of letters, new words. As the children progress in both their writing and reading/phonics skills, they will be able to add more words that rhyme with those given. Encourage their efforts. Move toward writing sentences and stories.
11. Praise all efforts.
12. Circle the best attempt for each letter and word.

Lesson 28 Name:

u u u u u u u u

u u

s s s s s s s s

s s

v w x y z

you us so see

Horizons® Penmanship Grade 1 59

Suggested Bible Verse Lessons 26-30:

"Who can ascend the hill of the Lord?
Who may stand in his holy place?"
(Psalm 24:3)

Lesson 29 - Review of Letters and Sequence, Punctuation

Teaching Tips:

1. Review letters and sequence: **s**, **t**, **u**, **v**, **w**, **x**, **y**, **z**.
2. Punctuation – Note punctuation on Bible verses and on sentences in lessons from other subjects.
3. (**.**) period: dot on the bottom line.
4. (**!**) exclamation point: two strokes – a long line that begins at the top of the second stage and ends just above the bottom of the booster. Pick up pencil and make a dot on the line just below.
5. (**?**) question mark: two strokes – a hook and a dot. Begin at 10 o'clock position, go up, around, and down just into the booster stage. Pick up the pencil and make a dot on the line just below the "hook."
6. (**.**) period: a dot on the bottom line.
7. (**,**) comma: a dot on the bottom line with a short, curved tail.
8. (**:**) colon: two dots – one on the dashed line and one directly underneath on the bottom line. Point out the differences between a colon and a semicolon. Show where these punctuation marks are used in future lessons.
9. (**;**) semicolon: a dot on the dashed line and a comma directly underneath.
10. Remind the students to write their first and last names on the top line.
11. Warm-up for each letter and check position.

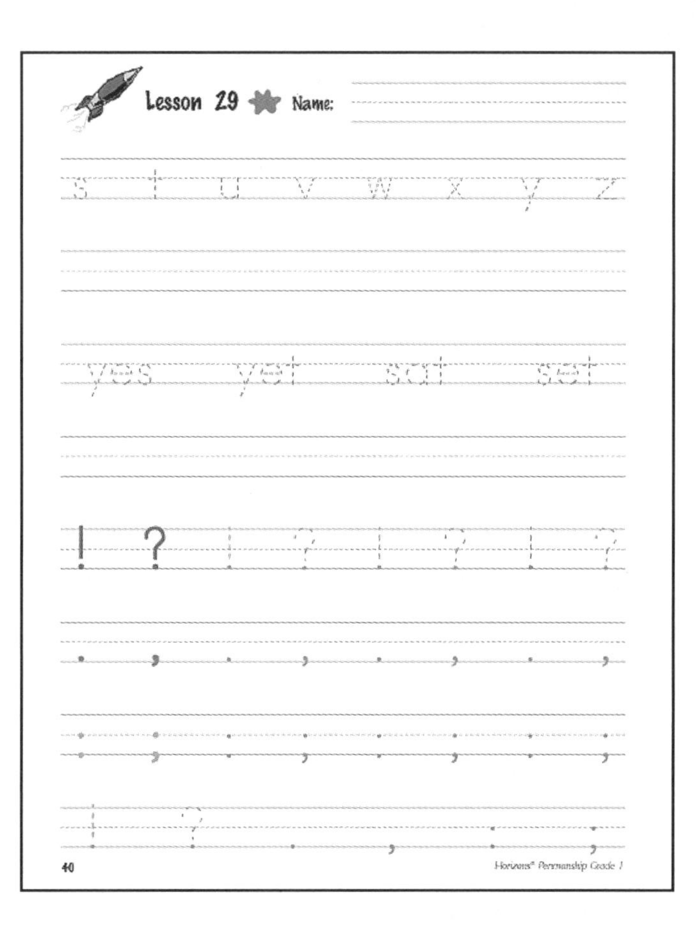

12. Have the students trace and copy the letters and punctuation marks while observing the position, formation, and spacing.
13. Give the children time to rest if needed.
14. Praise all efforts.
15. Circle the best attempt for each letter and word.

Suggested Bible Verse Lessons 26-30:

"Who can ascend the hill of the Lord? Who may stand in his holy place?"
(Psalm 24:3)

Lesson 30 - Numbers 6, 7, 8, 9, 10

Teaching Tips:

1. **6**: one stroke – top of the second stage, curve down to the bottom of the booster then around and up.
2. **7**: one stroke – across the top of the second stage and slant down and back to the bottom of the booster.
3. **8**: one stroke – begins very much like an "S" then back around.
4. **9**: one stroke – begins like a small circle in the second stage, then straight line up and down to the bottom of the booster.
5. **10**: two strokes – tall line and large oval. Note that the zero is slightly thinner than a capital "O."
6. Remind the children to write both their first and last names on the top line.
7. Warm-up and check position.
8. Have the students trace and copy the numbers while observing the position, formation, and spacing.
9. Give the children time to rest if needed.
10. Praise all efforts.
11. Circle the best attempt for each number.

Suggested Bible Verse Lessons 26-30:

"Who can ascend the hill of the Lord? Who may stand in his holy place?"
(Psalm 24:3)

Lesson 31 - Letters f, j, k

Teaching Tips:

1. **f**: two strokes – begin at 1 o'clock (second stage): and go up, around and straight down to the bottom of the booster; pick up pencil and make a short cross line on the dotted line.
2. **j**: two strokes – begin at the dotted line and go down through the booster and into tail, then around and up inside the tail (to the left) as in the small "g." Pick up pencil and make a dot in the middle of the second stage just above the letter.
3. **k**: two strokes – tall line through second stage and booster; two slanted lines into the tall one, beginning at the dotted line (booster stage).
4. Talk about the name and the sound each letter makes. Note how each letter is formed (use the rocket reference points).
5. Warm-up for each letter and check position.
6. Remind the children to write both their first and last names on the top line.
7. Have the students trace and copy the letters while observing the position, formation, and spacing.
8. Give the children time to rest if needed.
9. Introduce practice lines, sequences of letters, new words. As the children progress in both their writing and reading/phonics skills, they will be able to add more words that rhyme with those given. Encourage their efforts. Move toward writing sentences and stories.

10. Praise all efforts.
11. Circle the best attempt for each letter and word.

Suggested Bible Verse Lessons 31-35:

"How lovely is your dwelling place, O Lord Almighty!" (Psalm 84:1)

Lessons 32 and 33 - Review of All Lowercase Letters

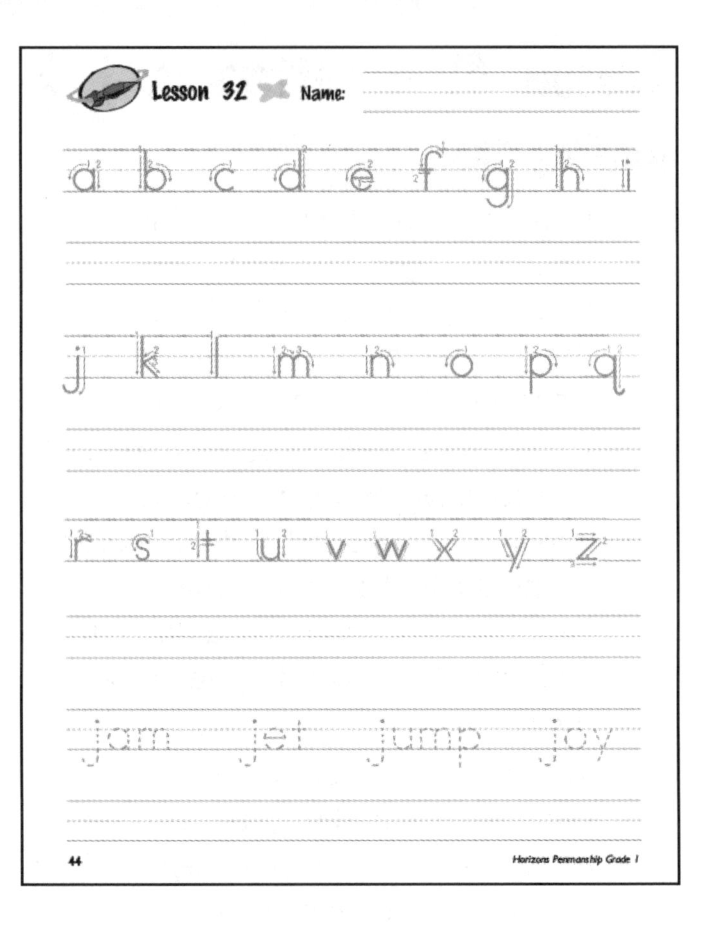

Teaching Tips:

1. Watch for any irregular formations or reversals.
2. Talk about the name and the sound each letter makes. Note how each letter is formed.
3. Warm-up for each letter and check position.
4. Remind the children to write both their first and last names on the top line.
5. Have the students trace and copy the letters while observing the position, formation, and spacing.
6. Give the children time to rest if needed.
7. Introduce practice lines, sequences of letters, new words. As the children progress in both their writing and reading/phonics skills, they will be able to add more words that rhyme with those given. Encourage their efforts. Move toward writing sentences and stories.
8. Praise all efforts.
9. Circle the best attempt for each letter and word.

Suggested Bible Verse Lessons 31-35:

"How lovely is your dwelling place, O Lord Almighty!" (Psalm 84:1)

Lesson 34 & 35 - Review of Words & Numbers

Teaching Tips:

1. The focus of the word review is proper formation and proper spacing between words.
2. Students are reviewing the correct formation of all numbers from 1–10.
3. Have students read each line of words.
4. Warm-up for each letter and check position.
5. Remind the children to write both their first and last names on the top line.
6. Have the students trace and say the words while observing the position, formation, and spacing.
7. Give the children time to rest if needed.
8. As the children progress in both their writing and reading/phonics skills, they will be able to add more words that rhyme with those given. Encourage their efforts. Move toward writing sentences and stories.
9. Praise all efforts.
10. Circle the best attempt for each word or number.

Suggested Bible Verse Lessons 31-35:

"How lovely is your dwelling place, O Lord Almighty!" (Psalm 84:1)

Lesson 34 Name:

do ad add dad

ace odd doe code

cab dab pad bad

go dog pod bag

it lit bit pit

mat hat bat pat

met pet rat art

ham man ran tan

46 Horizons® Penmanship Grade 1

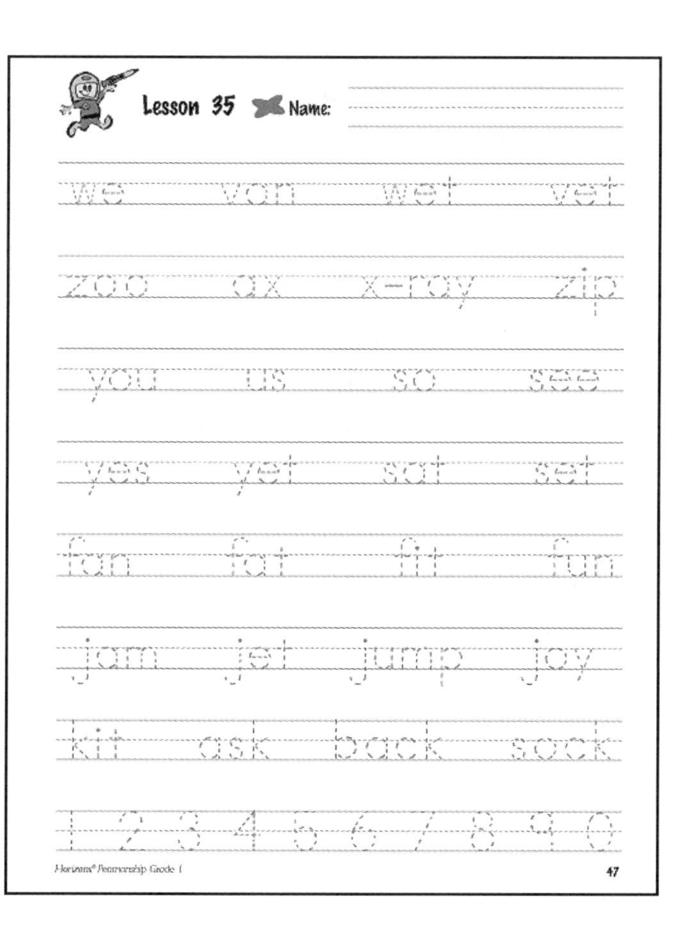

Lesson 35 Name:

we van wet vet

zoo ax x-ray zip

you us so see

yes yet sat set

fan fat fit fun

jam jet jump joy

kit ask back sock

1 2 3 4 5 6 7 8 9 0

Horizons® Penmanship Grade 1 47

Lesson 36 - Capital Letters O, C, G

Teaching Tips:

1. Introduce **I John 4:16**.
2. Letters: **O**, **C**, **G** – Note that all use both the second stage and booster. Review lowercase **o**, **c**, **g**.
3. **O**: Large circle, one stroke, begins at 2 o'clock, up, around, and back up.
4. **C**: One stroke, begins at 2 o'clock, up, around, and stops at 4 o'clock.
5. **G**: One stroke – begin at 2 o'clock, up, around, and at the dotted line draw a line across to the middle.
6. Words: stress that names like "God" and the first words of sentences begin with capital letters.
7. Talk about the name and the sound each letter makes. Note how each letter is formed (use the rocket reference points).
8. Warm-up for each letter and check position.
9. Remind the children to write both their first and last names on the top line.
10. Have the students trace and copy the letters while observing the position, formation, and spacing.
11. Give the children time to rest if needed.
12. Praise all efforts.
13. Circle the best attempt for each letter and word.

Bible Verse Lessons 36-40:

"God is love." (I John 4:16)

Lesson 37 - Capital Letters Q, J, D

Teaching Tips:

1. Letters: **Q**, **J**, **D** – all use both the second stage and the booster. Review lowercase **q**, **j**, **d**.
2. **Q**: Two strokes – large circle, slant line beginning in the middle of the booster stage and crossing the circle between the 5 and 6 o'clock position.
3. **J**: Two strokes: begin at the top of the second stage, straight down and around the bottom of the booster, flat top on top.
4. **D**: Two strokes – tall line down and large half circle.
5. Talk about the name and the sound each letter makes. Note how each letter is formed (use the rocket reference points).
6. Warm-up for each letter and check position.
7. Remind the children to write both their first and last names on the top line.
8. Have the students trace and copy the letters while observing the position, formation, and spacing.
9. Give the children time to rest if needed.
10. Praise all efforts.
11. Circle the best attempt for each letter and word.

Bible Verse Lessons 36-40:

"God is love." (I John 4:16)

Lesson 38 - Capital Letters P, B, R

Teaching Tips:

1. Letters: **P**, **B**, **R** – All use both the second stage and the booster. Review lowercase **p**, **b**, **r**.
2. **P**: Two strokes – tall line down and small loop at top (second stage). Note that the top of the "P" is slightly wider than a half circle.
3. **B**: Two strokes – tall line down and double loop (booster stage slightly larger than the second stage loop).
4. **R**: Two strokes – tall line down and combination of half loop in the second stage and slant line out in the booster stage (like a "P" with a cane).
5. Words: stress that proper nouns like "God" and the names of people begin with capital letters.
6. Talk about the name and the sound each letter makes. Note how each letter is formed (use the rocket reference points).
7. Warm-up for each letter and check position.
8. Remind the children to write both their first and last names on the top line.
9. Have the students trace and copy the letters while observing the position, formation, and spacing.
10. Give the children time to rest if needed.
11. Praise all efforts.
12. Circle the best attempt for each letter and word.

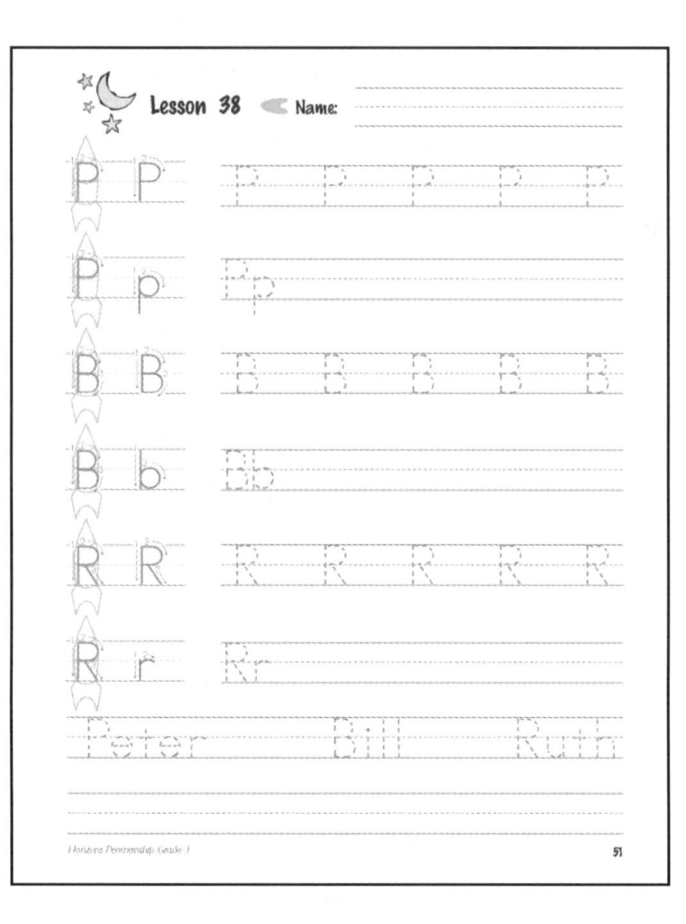

Bible Verse Lessons 36-40:

"God is love." (I John 4:16)

Lesson 39 - Practice Bible Verse

Teaching Tips:

1. Review **I John 4:16** with children.
2. Discuss meaning of verse and reading of the citation or Scripture reference.
3. Watch formation and spacing.
4. Children may further decorate the page if desired.
5. Have the students trace and copy the words while observing the position, formation, and spacing.
6. Give the children time to rest if needed.
7. Praise all efforts.
8. Circle the best attempt for each letter and word.

Bible Verse Lessons 36-40:

"God is love." (I John 4:16)

Lesson 40 - Special Page

Teaching Tips:

1. Explain that the children will copy the verse from Lesson 39 onto this special page using their best handwriting skills.
2. Remind the children to write both their first and last names on the top line.
3. Students requiring additional practice before writing the Bible verse may use the practice pages duplicated from the masters located in the back of this *Teacher's Guide*. There is a practice page for each of the Bible verse pages.
4. Complete the page, color, and decorate it.
5. Decide how this special page will be used.

Lesson 41 - Capital Letters V, W, X

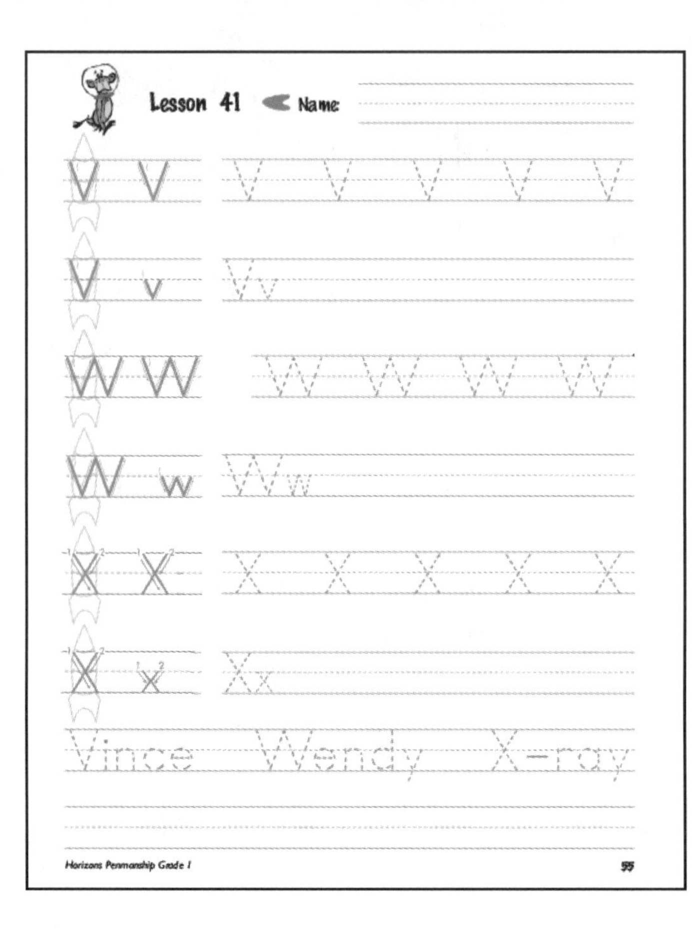
Lesson 41 Name

V V V V V V V

V v Vv

W W W W W W

W w Ww

X X X X X X X

X x Xx

Vince Wendy X-ray

Horizons Penmanship Grade 1 55

Teaching Tips:

1. Letters: **V**, **W**, **X** – Note that all letters are formed like their lowercase forms but are taller and use both the second stage and the booster of the rocket. Review lowercase **v**, **w**, **x**.
2. Strokes and formation as in lowercase letters.
3. Talk about the name and the sound each letter makes. Note how each letter is formed (use the rocket reference points).
4. Warm-up for each letter and check position.
5. Have the students trace and copy the letters while observing the position, formation, and spacing.
6. Give the children time to rest if needed.
7. Praise all efforts.
8. Circle the best attempt for each letter and word.

Bible Verse Lessons 41-45:

"Love your neighbor as yourself."
(Matthew 19:19)

Lesson 42 - Capital Letters Y, Z, A

Teaching Tips:

1. Letters: **Y**, **Z**, **A** – All letters use both the second stage and booster sections of the rocket. Review lowercase **y**, **z**, **a**.
2. **Y**: Three strokes – two slanted lines beginning at the top of the second stage and coming in to meet at the dotted line; a half-line straight down from the meeting point to the bottom line of the booster.
3. **Z**: Formation as to lowercase "z," beginning at the top of the second stage.
4. **A**: Three strokes – two tall, slanted lines meeting at the top of the second stage; a short line across the dotted line to join the two slanted lines.
5. Words: stress that proper nouns like "God" and the names of people begin with capital letters.
6. Talk about the name and the sound each letter makes. Note how each letter is formed (use the rocket reference points).
7. Warm-up for each letter and check position.
8. Have the students trace and copy the letters while observing the position, formation, and spacing.
9. Give the children time to rest if needed.
10. Praise all efforts.
11. Circle the best attempt for each letter and word.

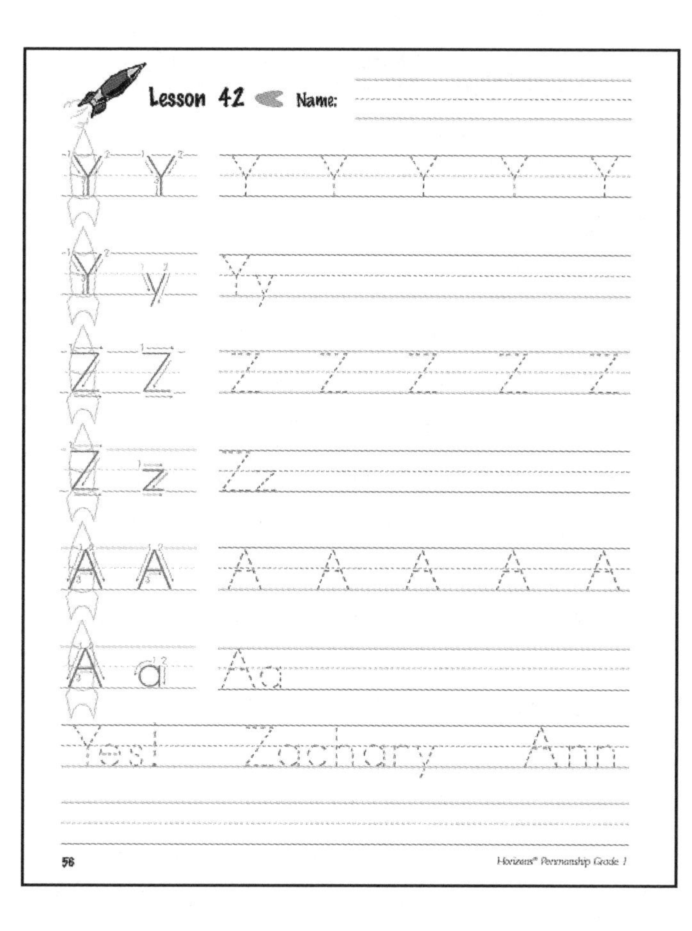
Lesson 42 Name:
Y Y Y Y Y Y Y
Y y Yy
Z Z Z Z Z Z Z
Z z Zz
A A A A A A A
A a Aa
Yes! Zachary Ann
58 Horizons® Penmanship Grade 1

Bible Verse Lessons 41-45:

"Love your neighbor as yourself."
(Matthew 19:19)

Lesson 43 - Capital Letters M, N, S

Teaching Tips:

1. Letters: **M**, **N**, **S** – All letters use both second stage and booster sections. Review lowercase **m**, **n**, **s**.
2. **M**: Two strokes – begin at the top and draw a tall line down, (lift) go back to top, slanted right to bottom, slant left to top, tall line down to bottom.
3. **N**: Two strokes – begin at the top and draw a tall line down, (lift) go back to top, slanted right to bottom, tall line up to top.
4. **S**: Formation as in lowercase "s."
5. Words: stress that proper nouns like "God" and the names of people begin with capital letters.
6. Talk about the name and the sound each letter makes. Note how each letter is formed (use the rocket reference points).
7. Warm-up for each letter and check position.
8. Remind the children to write both their first and last names on the top line.
9. Have the students trace and copy the letters while observing the position, formation, and spacing.
10. Give the children time to rest if needed.
11. Praise all efforts.
12. Circle the best attempt for each letter and word.

Lesson 43 Name:

M M M M M M M

M m Mm

N N N N N N N

N n Nn

S S S S S S S

S s Ss

Mary Nancy Sam

Horizons Penmanship Grade 1 57

Bible Verse Lessons 41-45:

"Love your neighbor as yourself."
(Matthew 19:19)

Lesson 44 - Practice Bible Verse

Teaching Tips:

1. Review **Matthew 19:19** with children.
2. Discuss meaning of verse and reading of the citation or Scripture reference.
3. Watch formation and spacing.
4. Children may decorate page as practice.
5. Have the students trace and copy the words while observing the position, formation, spacing and punctuation.
6. Give the children time to rest if needed.
7. Praise all efforts.
8. Circle the best attempt for each letter and word.

Bible Verse Lessons 41-45:

"Love your neighbor as yourself."
(Matthew 19:19)

Lesson 45 - Special Page

Teaching Tips:

1. Explain that the children will copy the verse from Lesson 40 onto this special page using their best handwriting skills.
2. Students requiring additional practice before writing the Bible verse may use the practice pages duplicated from the masters located in the back of this *Teacher's Guide*. There is a practice page for each of the Bible verse pages.
3. Complete the page and finish decorating it.
4. Decide how this special page will be used.

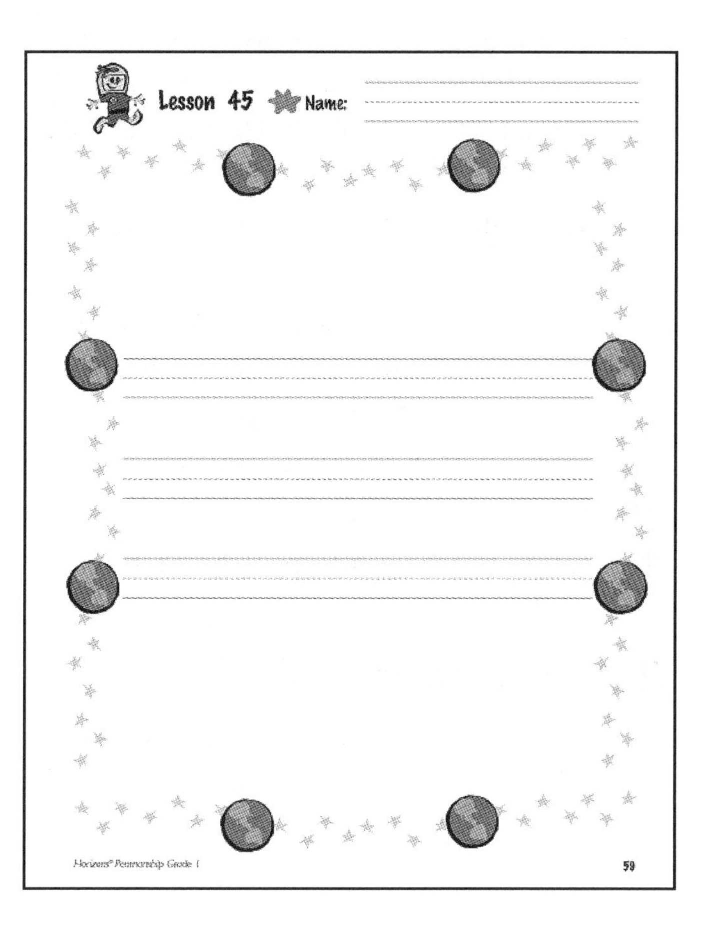

Lesson 46 - Capital Letters E, F, H

Teaching Tips:

1. Letters: **E**, **F**, **H** – All use both second stage and booster. Review lowercase **e**, **f**, **h**.
2. **E**: Four strokes – one tall line, three short lines out from the tall line: top line across, dotted line across, bottom line across.
3. **F**: Three strokes – one tall line, two short lines out from the tall line; top line across, dotted line across.
4. **H**: Three strokes – two tall lines separated (goal posts), one line across the dotted line to join the two tall lines.
5. Words: stress that the names of people begin with capital letters.
6. Talk about the name and the sound each letter makes. Note how each letter is formed (use the rocket reference points).
7. Warm-up for each letter and check position.
8. Have the students trace and copy the letters while observing the position, formation, and spacing.
9. Give the children time to rest if needed.
10. Praise all efforts.
11. Circle the best attempt for each letter and word.

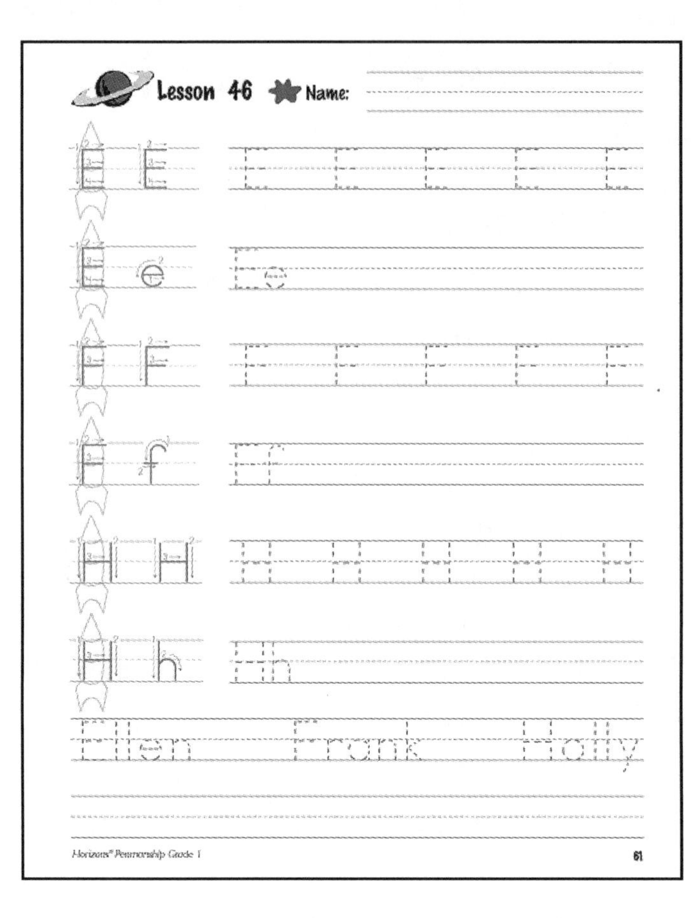

Bible Verse Lessons 46-50:

"Keep me safe, O God, for in you I take refuge." (Psalm 16:1)

Lesson 47 - Capital Letters T, I, L

Teaching Tips:

1. Letters: **T**, **I**, **L** – All use both second stage and booster. Review lowercase **t**, **i**, **l**.
2. **T**: Two strokes – one tall line, one short line across the top.
3. **I**: Three strokes – one tall line, two short Lines—one across the top, one across the bottom.
4. **L**: One stroke – one tall line moving into a short line out from the bottom.
5. Talk about the name and the sound each letter makes. Note how each letter is formed (use the rocket reference points).
6. Words: stress that the names of people begin with capital letters.
7. Warm-up for each letter and check position.
8. Have the students trace and copy the letters while observing the position, formation, and spacing.
9. Give the children time to rest if needed.
10. Praise all efforts.
11. Circle the best attempt for each letter and word.

Bible Verse Lessons 46-50:

"Keep me safe, O God, for in you I take refuge." (Psalm 16:1)

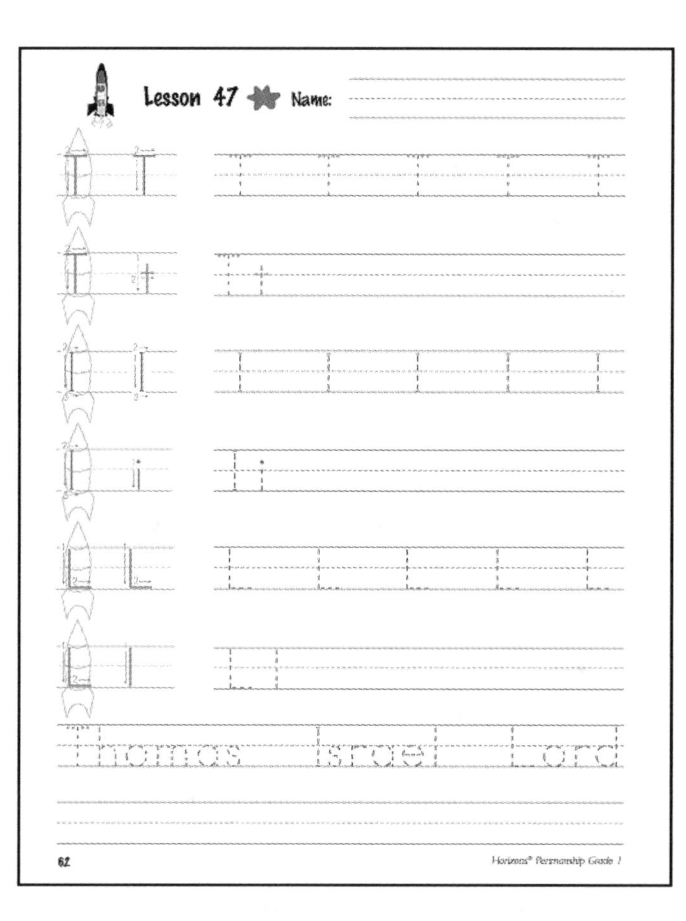

Lesson 48 - Capital Letters K & U

Teaching Tips:

1. Letters: **K**, **U** – All use both second stage and booster. Review lowercase **k**, **u**.
2. **K**: Two strokes – one tall line, two slanted lines (top into the middle of the tall line, then back out to the bottom line).
3. **U**: One stroke – begin as tall line, down, around, and back up to the top line.
4. Talk about the name and the sound each letter makes. Note how each letter is formed (use the rocket reference points).
5. Warm-up for each letter and check position.
6. Words: stress that the names of people begin with capital letters.
7. Have the students trace and copy the letters while observing the position, formation, and spacing.
8. Give the children time to rest if needed.
9. Praise all efforts.
10. Circle the best attempt for each letter and word.

Bible Verse Lessons 46-50:

"Keep me safe, O God, for in you I take refuge." (Psalm 16:1)

Lesson 48 Name:

K K K K K K K

K k Kk

U U U U U U U

U u Uu

Kathy Uriah

Keep safe refuge

Horizons® Penmanship Grade 1 63

Lessons 49-50 - Bible Verse Practice & Special Page

Teaching Tips:

1. Review **Psalm 16:1** with children.
2. Discuss meaning of verse and reading of the citation or Scripture reference.
3. Remind the children to write both their first and last names on the top line.
4. Watch formation and spacing.
5. Children may decorate page as practice.
6. Have the students trace and copy the words while observing the position, formation, spacing and punctuation.
7. Give the children time to rest if needed.
8. Praise all efforts.
9. Explain that the children will copy the verse from Lesson 49 onto this special page using their best handwriting skills.
10. Complete the page and decorate it.
11. Decide how this special page will be used.
12. Children requiring additional practice may use the practice pages duplicated from the masters located in the back of the *Teacher's Guide*.

Bible Verse Lessons 46-50:

"Keep me safe, O God, for in you I take refuge." (Psalm 16:1)

Lessons 51-52 - Tracing Practice of Capital & Lowercase Letters

Teaching Tips:

1. Talk about the name and the sound each letter makes. Note how each letter is formed.
2. Warm-up for each letter and check position.
3. Have the students trace and copy the letters while observing the position, formation, and spacing.
4. Give the children time to rest if needed.
5. Children may gain additional practice in writing capital and lowercase letters by using practice pages duplicated from the masters located in the back of the *Teacher's Guide*.
6. Praise all efforts.
7. Circle the best attempt for each letter and word.

Bible Verse Lessons 51-55:

"Give thanks to the Lord, for he is good."
(Psalm 106:1)

Lesson 51 Name:

A A B B C C D D
E E F F G G
H H I I J J K K
L L M M N N
O O P P Q Q
R R S S T T
U U V V W W
X X Y Y Z Z

Horizons® Penmanship Grade 1 67

Lesson 52 Name:

a a b b c c d d
e e f f g g
h h i i j j k k
l l m m n n
o o p p q q
r r s s t t
u u v v w w
x x y y z z

68 Horizons® Penmanship Grade 1

Lesson 53 - Bible Verse Practice

Teaching Tips:

1. Review **Psalm 106:1** with the students and discuss the meaning of the verse. Ask the children what it means to be thankful and have them name some things they are thankful for.
2. Practice words and spacing of words and phrases from the Bible verse for the week.
3. Warm-up and check position.
4. Have the students trace and copy the words while observing the position, formation, and spacing.
5. Give the children time to rest if needed.
6. Children requiring additional practice may use the practice pages duplicated from the masters located in the back of the *Teacher's Guide*.
7. Praise all efforts.
8. Circle the best attempt for each letter and word.

Bible Verse Lessons 51-55:

"Give thanks to the Lord, for he is good."
(Psalm 106:1)

Lesson 53 Name:

Give thanks

to the Lord,

for he

is good.

Horizons® Penmanship Grade 1 69

Lessons 54-55 - Bible Verse Practice & Special Page

Teaching Tips:

1. Do warm-up activities.
2. On these pages the children will not only practice the Bible verse but will have the opportunity to show their best work on a special page that they can take home or display in the classroom.
3. Have the children take their time. Emphasize the spacing needed between words and make sure they include all necessary punctuation.
4. Encourage the children to stop if their hands become tired and rest for a minute.
5. Allow them to further decorate the pages if they choose.
6. Talk about sharing God's Word with others. Stress the importance of being able to write to others about God and being able to share His Word with them.
7. Discuss ways in which the special page can be used.
8. Children requiring additional practice may use the practice pages duplicated from the masters located in the back of the *Teacher's Guide*.

Bible Verse Lessons 51-55:

"Give thanks to the Lord, for he is good."
(Psalm 106:1)

Lesson 56 - Introduce Sentence Elements

Teaching Tips:

1. Review and individual practice for letters: **Aa**, **Bb**, **Mm**.
2. Talk about the name and the sound each letter makes. Note how each letter is formed.
3. Warm-up for each letter and check position.
4. Have the students trace and copy the letters while observing the position, formation, and spacing.
5. Give the children time to rest if needed.
6. Children requiring additional practice may use the practice pages duplicated from the masters located in the back of the *Teacher's Guide*.
7. Praise all efforts.
8. Circle the best attempt for each letter and word.
9. Introduce sentence elements: a capital letter at the beginning, appropriate punctuation at the end, and making sure the sentence expresses a complete thought.
10. Give some examples of very short complete and incomplete sentences on the white board or chalkboard.
11. Stress that the names of people begin with capital letters.

Bible Verse Lessons 56-60:

"Blessed are the poor in spirit."
(Matthew 5:3)

Lesson 56 Name:

Aa Aa

Bb Bb

Mm Mm

Mary saw Ann and Bob.

Horizons® Penmanship Grade 1 73

Lessons 57-58 - Bible Verse Practice

Teaching Tips:

1. Review **Matthew 5:3** with the students and discuss the meaning of the verse. Ask the children what they think it means to be poor in spirit. Share with the children that the word "blessed" also means "happy."
2. Practice words and spacing of words and phrases from the Bible verse for the week.
3. Warm-up and check position.
4. Have the students trace and copy the words while observing the position, formation, and spacing.
5. Discuss the meaning of the sentences if desired.
6. Give the children time to rest if needed.
7. Children requiring additional practice may use the practice pages duplicated from the masters located in the back of the *Teacher's Guide*.
8. Praise all efforts.
9. Circle the best attempt for each letter and word.

Bible Verse Lessons 56-60:

"Blessed are the poor in spirit."
(Matthew 5:3)

Lesson 57 Name:

Blessed

are

the

Blessed be God!

74 Horizons® Penmanship Grade 1

Lesson 58 Name:

poor

in

spirit

God loves the poor.

Horizons® Penmanship Grade 1 75

Lessons 59-60 - Bible Verse Practice & Special Page

Teaching Tips:

1. Do warm-up activities and review the meaning of the Bible verse.
2. On these pages the children will not only practice the Bible verse but will have the opportunity to show their best work on a special page that they can take home or display in the classroom.
3. Have the children take their time. Emphasize the spacing needed between words and make sure they include all necessary punctuation.
4. Encourage the children to stop if their hands become tired and rest for a minute.
5. Allow them to further decorate the pages if they choose.
6. Talk about sharing God's Word with others. Stress the importance of being able to write to others about God and being able to share His Word with them.
7. Discuss ways in which the special page can be used.
8. Children requiring additional practice may use the practice pages duplicated from the masters located in the back of the *Teacher's Guide*.

Bible Verse Lessons 56-60:

"Blessed are the poor in spirit."
(Matthew 5:3)

Lesson 61 - Review Letters Cc, Ll & Jj

Teaching Tips:

1. Review and individual practice for letters: **Cc**, **Ll**, **Jj**.
2. Talk about the name and the sound each letter makes. Note how each letter is formed.
3. Warm-up for each letter and check position.
4. Have the students trace and copy the letters while observing the position, formation, and spacing.
5. Discuss the meaning of the sentence if desired.
6. Give the children time to rest if needed.
7. Praise all efforts.
8. Circle the best attempt for each letter and word.
9. Children requiring additional practice may use the practice pages duplicated from the masters located in the back of the *Teacher's Guide*.

Bible Verse Lessons 61-65:

"Come, Lord Jesus." (Revelation 22:20)

Lesson 61 Name:

Cc Cc

Ll Ll

Jj Jj

The Lord Jesus saves us.

Horizons® Penmanship Grade 1 79

Lessons 62-63 - Bible Verse & Letter Practice

Teaching Tips:

1. Review **Revelation 22:20** with the students and discuss the meaning of the verse.
2. Practice words and spacing of words and phrases from the Bible verse for the week.
3. Review and individual practice for the letter **Rr**.
4. Warm-up and check position.
5. Have the students trace and copy the words while observing the position, formation, and spacing.
6. Discuss the meaning of the sentences if desired.
7. Give the children time to rest if needed.
8. Children requiring additional practice may use the practice pages duplicated from the masters located in the back of the *Teacher's Guide*.
9. Praise all efforts.
10. Circle the best attempt for each letter and word.

Bible Verse Lessons 61-65:

"Come, Lord Jesus." (Revelation 22:20)

Lesson 62 Name:

Come

Lord

Jesus comes

into our hearts.

80 Horizons® Penmanship Grade 1

Lesson 63 Name:

Rr Rr

Revelation

John wrote the

book of Revelation.

Horizons® Penmanship Grade 1 81

Lessons 64-65 - Bible Verse Practice & Special Page

Teaching Tips:

1. Do warm-up activities and review the meaning of the Bible verse.
2. On these pages the children will not only practice the Bible verse but will have the opportunity to show their best work on a special page that they can take home or display in the classroom.
3. Have the children take their time. Emphasize the spacing needed between words and make sure they include all necessary punctuation.
4. Encourage the children to stop if their hands become tired and rest for a minute.
5. Allow them to further decorate the pages if they choose.
6. Talk about sharing God's Word with others. Stress the importance of being able to write to others about God and being able to share His Word with them.
7. Discuss ways in which the special page can be used.
8. Children requiring additional practice may use the practice pages duplicated from the masters located in the back of the *Teacher's Guide*.

Bible Verse Lessons 61-65:

"Come, Lord Jesus." (Revelation 22:20)

Lesson 66 - Review Letters Dd, Gg & Ff

Teaching Tips:

1. Review and individual practice for letters: **Dd**, **Gg**, **Ff**.
2. Talk about the name and the sound each letter makes. Note how each letter is formed.
3. Warm-up for each letter and check position.
4. Have the students trace and copy the letters while observing the position, formation, and spacing.
5. Discuss the meaning of the sentence if desired.
6. Give the children time to rest if needed.
7. Praise all efforts.
8. Circle the best attempt for each letter and word.
9. Children requiring additional practice may use the practice pages duplicated from the masters located in the back of the *Teacher's Guide*.

Bible Verse Lessons 66-70:

"Glory to God in the highest, and on earth peace to men on whom His favor rests."
(Luke 2:14)

Lessons 67-68 - Bible Verse Practice

Teaching Tips:

1. Review **Luke 2:14** with the students and discuss the meaning of the verse.
2. Practice words and spacing of words and phrases from the Bible verse for the week.
3. Warm-up and check position.
4. Have the students trace and copy the words while observing the position, formation, and spacing.
5. Discuss the meaning of the sentence if desired.
6. Give the children time to rest if needed.
7. Children requiring additional practice may use the practice pages duplicated from the masters located in the back of the *Teacher's Guide*.
8. Praise all efforts.
9. Circle the best attempt for each word.

Bible Verse Lessons 66-70:

"Glory to God in the highest, and on earth peace to men on whom His favor rests."

(Luke 2:14)

Lesson 67 Name:

Glory

God

favor

Give God glory!

86 Horizons® Penmanship Grade 1

Lesson 68 Name:

highest

peace

earth

Pray for peace on earth.

Horizons® Penmanship Grade 1 87

Lessons 69-70 - Bible Verse Practice & Special Page

Teaching Tips:

1. Do warm-up activities and review the meaning of the Bible verse.
2. On these pages the children will not only practice the Bible verse but will have the opportunity to show their best work on a special page that they can take home or display in the classroom.
3. Have the children take their time. Emphasize the spacing needed between words and make sure they include all necessary punctuation.
4. Encourage the children to stop if their hands become tired and rest for a minute.
5. Allow them to further decorate the pages if they choose.
6. Talk about sharing God's Word with others. Stress the importance of being able to write to others about God and being able to share His Word with them.
7. Discuss ways in which the special page can be used.
8. Children requiring additional practice may use the practice pages duplicated from the masters located in the back of the *Teacher's Guide*.

Bible Verse Lessons 66-70:

"Glory to God in the highest, and on earth peace to men on whom His favor rests."
(Luke 2:14)

Lesson 71 - Review Letters Ee, Hh & Tt

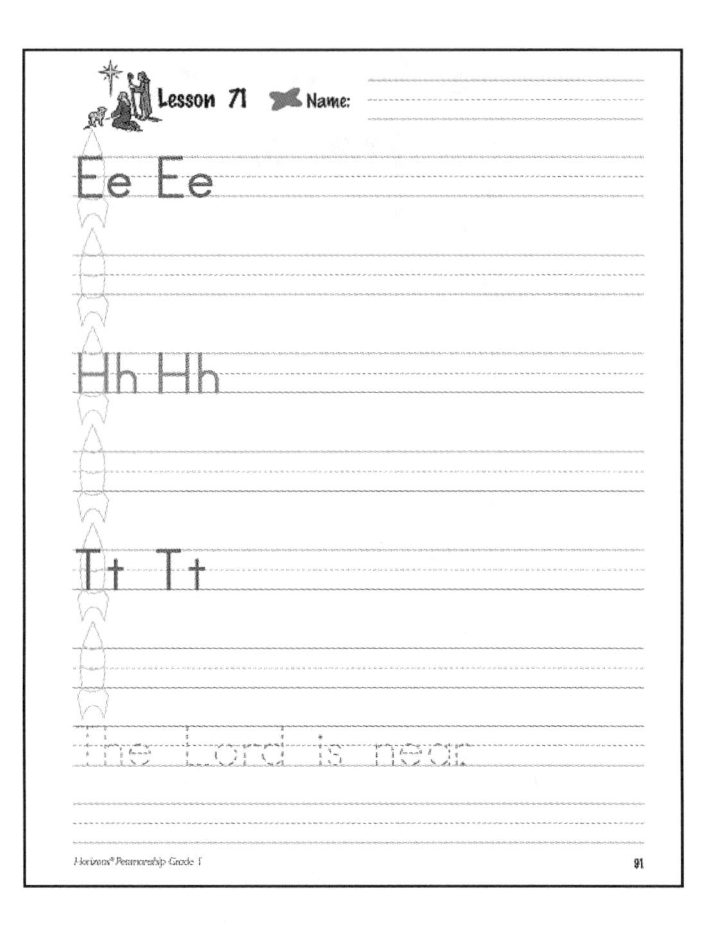

Teaching Tips:

1. Review and individual practice for letters: **Ee**, **Hh**, **Tt**.
2. Talk about the name and the sound each letter makes. Note how each letter is formed.
3. Warm-up for each letter and check position.
4. Have the students trace and copy the letters while observing the position, formation, and spacing.
5. Discuss the meaning of the sentence if desired.
6. Give the children time to rest if needed.
7. Praise all efforts.
8. Circle the best attempt for each letter and word.
9. Children requiring additional practice may use the practice pages duplicated from the masters located in the back of the *Teacher's Guide*.

Bible Verse Lessons 71-75:

"The shepherds found Mary and Joseph, and the baby, who was lying in a manger."
(Luke 2:16)

Lessons 72-73 - Bible Verse Practice

Teaching Tips:

1. Review **Luke 2:16** with the students and discuss the meaning of the verse.
2. Practice words and spacing of words and phrases from the Bible verse for the week.
3. Warm-up and check position.
4. Have the students trace and copy the words while observing the position, formation, and spacing.
5. Discuss the meaning of the sentence if desired.
6. Give the children time to rest if needed.
7. Children requiring additional practice may use the practice pages duplicated from the masters located in the back of the *Teacher's Guide*.
8. Praise all efforts.
9. Circle the best attempt for each word.

Bible Verse Lessons 71-75:

"The shepherds found Mary and Joseph, and the baby, who was lying in a manger."
(Luke 2:16)

Lesson 72 Name:

shepherds

baby

manger

The shepherds saw

the baby Jesus.

92 Horizons® Penmanship Grade 1

Lesson 73 Name:

Mary

Joseph

found

Mary and Joseph

loved Jesus.

Horizons® Penmanship Grade 1 93

Lessons 74-75 - Bible Verse Practice & Special Page

Teaching Tips:

1. Do warm-up activities and review the meaning of the Bible verse.
2. On these pages the children will not only practice the Bible verse but will have the opportunity to show their best work on a special page that they can take home or display in the classroom.
3. Have the children take their time. Emphasize the spacing needed between words and make sure they include all necessary punctuation.
4. Encourage the children to stop if their hands become tired and rest for a minute.
5. Allow them to further decorate the pages if they choose.
6. Talk about sharing God's Word with others. Stress the importance of being able to write to others about God and being able to share His Word with them.
7. Discuss ways in which the special page can be used.
8. Children requiring additional practice may use the practice pages duplicated from the masters located in the back of the *Teacher's Guide*.

Bible Verse Lessons 71-75:

"The shepherds found Mary and Joseph, and the baby, who was lying in a manger."
(Luke 2:16)

Lesson 76 - Review Letters Ii, Kk & Nn

Teaching Tips:

1. Review and individual practice for letters: **Ii**, **Kk**, **Nn**.
2. Talk about the name and the sound each letter makes. Note how each letter is formed.
3. Warm-up for each letter and check position.
4. Have the students trace and copy the letters while observing the position, formation, and spacing.
5. Discuss the meaning of the sentence if desired.
6. Give the children time to rest if needed.
7. Praise all efforts.
8. Circle the best attempt for each letter and word.
9. Children requiring additional practice may use the practice pages duplicated from the masters located in the back of the *Teacher's Guide*.

Bible Verse Lessons 76-80:

"Arise, shine, for your light has come."
(Isaiah 60:1)

Lesson 76 Name:

Ii Ii

Kk Kk

Nn Nn

Isaiah was a prophet.

Horizons Penmanship Grade 1 97

Lessons 77-78 - Bible Verse Practice

Teaching Tips:

1. Review **Isaiah 60:1** with the students and discuss the meaning of the verse.
2. Practice words and spacing of words and phrases from the Bible verse for the week.
3. Warm-up and check position.
4. Have the students trace and copy the words while observing the position, formation, and spacing.
5. Discuss the meaning of the sentences if desired.
6. Give the children time to rest if needed.
7. Children requiring additional practice may use the practice pages duplicated from the masters located in the back of the *Teacher's Guide*.
8. Praise all efforts.
9. Circle the best attempt for each word.

Bible Verse Lessons 76-80:

"Arise, shine, for your light has come."
(Isaiah 60:1)

Lesson 77 Name:

Arise

shine

light

Jesus is our light.

98 Horizons® Penmanship Grade 1

Lesson 78 Name:

your

come

Isaiah

Let your light shine.

Horizons® Penmanship Grade 1 99

Lessons 79-80 - Bible Verse Practice & Special Page

Teaching Tips:

1. Do warm-up activities and review the meaning of the Bible verse.
2. On these pages the children will not only practice the Bible verse but will have the opportunity to show their best work on a special page that they can take home or display in the classroom.
3. Have the children take their time. Emphasize the spacing needed between words and make sure they include all necessary punctuation.
4. Encourage the children to stop if their hands become tired and rest for a minute.
5. Allow them to further decorate the pages if they choose.
6. Talk about sharing God's Word with others. Stress the importance of being able to write to others about God and being able to share His Word with them.
7. Discuss ways in which the special page can be used.
8. Children requiring additional practice may use the practice pages duplicated from the masters located in the back of the *Teacher's Guide*.

Bible Verse Lessons 76-80:

"Arise, shine, for your light has come."
(Isaiah 60:1)

Lesson 81 - Review Letters Aa-Tt

Teaching Tips:

1. Review and individual practice for letters: **Aa** through **Tt**.
2. Talk about the name and the sound each letter makes. Note how each letter is formed.
3. Warm-up for each letter and check position.
4. Have the students trace and copy the letters while observing the position, formation, and spacing.
5. Give the children time to rest if needed.
6. Praise all efforts.
7. Circle the best attempt for each letter.
8. Children requiring additional practice may use the practice pages duplicated from the masters located in the back of the *Teacher's Guide*.

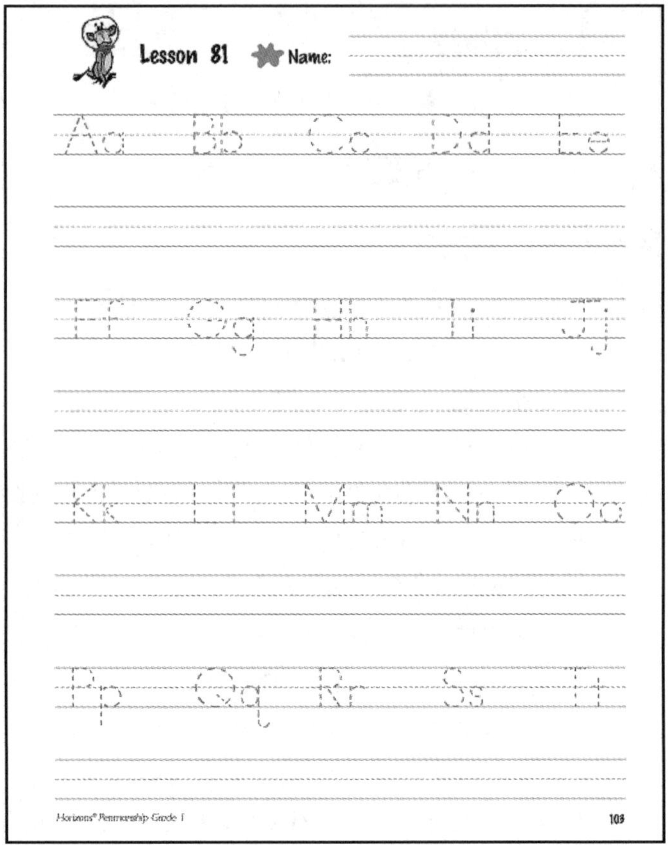

Bible Verse Lessons 81-85:

"Come to me, all you who are weary and burdened, and I will give you rest."
(Matthew 11:28)

Lessons 82-83 - Review Letters Uu-Zz & Bible Verse Practice

Teaching Tips:

1. Review and individual practice for letters: **Uu** through **Zz**.
2. Talk about the name and the sound each letter makes. Note how each letter is formed.
3. Warm-up for each letter and check position.
4. Have the students trace and copy the letters while observing the position, formation, and spacing.
5. Review **Matthew 11:28** with the students and discuss the meaning of the verse.
6. Practice words and spacing of words and phrases from the Bible verse for the week while observing the position, formation, spacing and punctuation.
7. Give the children time to rest if needed.
8. Children requiring additional practice may use the practice pages duplicated from the masters located in the back of the *Teacher's Guide*.
9. Praise all efforts.
10. Circle the best attempt for each word.

Bible Verse Lessons 81-85:

"Come to me, all you who are weary and burdened, and I will give you rest."
(Matthew 11:28)

Lesson 82 Name:

Uu Vv Ww Xx

Yy Zz Yy Zz

weary

burdened

104 Horizons® Penmanship Grade 1

Lesson 83 Name:

Come to me,

all you who are

weary and burdened,

and I will give you rest.

Horizons® Penmanship Grade 1 105

Lessons 84-85 - Bible Verse Practice & Special Page

Teaching Tips:

1. Do warm-up activities and review the meaning of the Bible verse.
2. On these pages the children will not only practice the Bible verse but will have the opportunity to show their best work on a special page that they can take home or display in the classroom.
3. Have the children take their time. Emphasize the spacing needed between words and make sure they include all necessary punctuation.
4. Encourage the children to stop if their hands become tired and rest for a minute.
5. Allow them to further decorate the pages if they choose.
6. Talk about sharing God's Word with others. Stress the importance of being able to write to others about God and being able to share His Word with them.
7. Discuss ways in which the special page can be used.
8. Children requiring additional practice may use the practice pages duplicated from the masters located in the back of the *Teacher's Guide*.

Bible Verse Lessons 81-85:

"Come to me, all you who are weary and burdened, and I will give you rest."
(Matthew 11:28)

Lesson 86 - Review Letters Oo, Pp & Qq

Teaching Tips:

1. Review and individual practice for letters: **Oo**, **Pp**, **Qq**.
2. Talk about the name and the sound each letter makes. Note how each letter is formed.
3. Warm-up for each letter and check position.
4. Have the students trace and copy the letters while observing the position, formation, and spacing.
5. Discuss the meaning of the sentence if desired.
6. Give the children time to rest if needed.
7. Praise all efforts.
8. Circle the best attempt for each letter.
9. Children requiring additional practice may use the practice pages duplicated from the masters located in the back of the *Teacher's Guide*.

Bible Verse Lessons 86-90:

"I will praise you, O Lord, with all my heart."
(Psalm 138:1)

Lesson 86 Name:

Oo Oo

Pp Pp

Qq Qq

I will praise the Lord.

Horizons® Penmanship Grade 1 109

Lessons 87-88 - Bible Verse Practice

Teaching Tips:

1. Review **Psalm 138:1** with the students and discuss the meaning of the verse.
2. Practice words and spacing of words and phrases from the Bible verse for the week.
3. Warm-up and check position.
4. Have the students trace and copy the words while observing the position, formation, and spacing.
5. Discuss the meaning of the sentences if desired.
6. Give the children time to rest if needed.
7. Children requiring additional practice may use the practice pages duplicated from the masters located in the back of the *Teacher's Guide*.
8. Praise all efforts.
9. Circle the best attempt for each word.

Bible Verse Lessons 86-90:

"I will praise you, O Lord, with all my heart."
(Psalm 138:1)

Lesson 87 Name:

Lord

heart

My heart will

praise the Lord.

110 Horizons® Penmanship Grade 1

Lesson 88 Name:

Psalm

praise

with all my heart

Psalms praise the Lord.

Horizons® Penmanship Grade 1 111

Lessons 89-90 - Bible Verse Practice & Special Page

Teaching Tips:

1. Do warm-up activities and review the meaning of the Bible verse.
2. On these pages the children will not only practice the Bible verse but will have the opportunity to show their best work on a special page that they can take home or display in the classroom.
3. Have the children take their time. Emphasize the spacing needed between words and make sure they include all necessary punctuation.
4. Encourage the children to stop if their hands become tired and rest for a minute.
5. Allow them to further decorate the pages if they choose.
6. Talk about sharing God's Word with others. Stress the importance of being able to write to others about God and being able to share His Word with them.
7. Discuss ways in which the special page can be used.
8. Children requiring additional practice may use the practice pages duplicated from the masters located in the back of the *Teacher's Guide*.

Bible Verse Lessons 86-90:

"I will praise you, O Lord, with all my heart."
(Psalm 138:1)

Lesson 91 - Review Letters Rr, Ss & Uu

Teaching Tips:

1. Review and individual practice for letters: **Rr**, **Ss**, **Uu**.
2. Talk about the name and the sound each letter makes. Note how each letter is formed.
3. Warm-up for each letter and check position.
4. Have the students trace and copy the letters while observing the position, formation, and spacing.
5. The last two blank lines may be used for additional letter practice or the student may write his or her own sentence if desired.
6. Give the children time to rest if needed.
7. Praise all efforts.
8. Circle the best attempt for each letter.
9. Children requiring additional practice may use the practice pages duplicated from the masters located in the back of the *Teacher's Guide*.

Bible Verse Lessons 91-95:

"Jesus, remember me when you come into your kingdom." (Luke 23:42)

Lesson 91 Name:

Rr Rr

Ss Ss

Uu Uu

Horizons® Penmanship Grade 1 115

Lessons 92-93 - Bible Verse Practice

Teaching Tips:

1. Review **Luke 23:42** with the students and discuss the meaning of the verse.
2. Practice words and spacing of words and phrases from the Bible verse for the week.
3. Warm-up and check position.
4. Have the students trace and copy the words while observing the position, formation, and spacing.
5. Discuss the meaning of the sentences if desired.
6. Give the children time to rest if needed.
7. Children requiring additional practice may use the practice pages duplicated from the masters located in the back of the *Teacher's Guide*.
8. Praise all efforts.
9. Circle the best attempt for each word.

Bible Verse Lessons 91-95:

"Jesus, remember me when you come into your kingdom." (Luke 23:42)

Lesson 92 Name:

remember

when

kingdom

Remember me, Jesus.

116 Horizons® Penmanship Grade 1

Lesson 93 Name:

Luke

Come into my kingdom.

Let me come

into your kingdom.

Horizons® Penmanship Grade 1 117

Lessons 94-95 - Bible Verse Practice & Special Page

Teaching Tips:

1. Do warm-up activities and review the meaning of the Bible verse.
2. On these pages the children will not only practice the Bible verse but will have the opportunity to show their best work on a special page that they can take home or display in the classroom.
3. Have the children take their time. Emphasize the spacing needed between words and make sure they include all necessary punctuation.
4. Encourage the children to stop if their hands become tired and rest for a minute.
5. Allow them to further decorate the pages if they choose.
6. Talk about sharing God's Word with others. Stress the importance of being able to write to others about God and being able to share His Word with them.
7. Discuss ways in which the special page can be used.
8. Children requiring additional practice may use the practice pages duplicated from the masters located in the back of the *Teacher's Guide*.

Bible Verse Lessons 91-95:

"Jesus, remember me when you come into your kingdom." (Luke 23:42)

Lesson 96 - Review Letters Vv, Ww & Xx

Teaching Tips:

1. Review and individual practice for letters: **Vv**, **Ww**, **Xx**.
2. Talk about the name and the sound each letter makes. Note how each letter is formed.
3. Warm-up for each letter and check position.
4. Have the students trace and copy the letters while observing the position, formation, and spacing.
5. The last two blank lines may be used for additional letter practice or the student may write his or her own sentence if desired.
6. Give the children time to rest if needed.
7. Praise all efforts.
8. Circle the best attempt for each letter.
9. Children requiring additional practice may use the practice pages duplicated from the masters located in the back of the *Teacher's Guide*.

Bible Verse Lessons 96-100:

"Father, into your hands I commend my Spirit." (Luke 23:46)

Lesson 96 Name:

Vv Vv

Ww Ww

Xx Xx

Horizons® Penmanship Grade 1 121

Lessons 97-98 - Bible Verse Practice

Teaching Tips:

1. Review **Luke 23:46** with the students and discuss the meaning of the verse.
2. Practice words and spacing of words and phrases from the Bible verse for the week.
3. Warm-up and check position.
4. Have the students trace and copy the words while observing the position, formation, spacing and punctuation.
5. Give the children time to rest if needed.
6. Children requiring additional practice may use the practice pages duplicated from the masters located in the back of the *Teacher's Guide*.
7. Praise all efforts.
8. Circle the best attempt for each word.

Bible Verse Lessons 96-100:

"Father, into your hands I commend my Spirit." (Luke 23:46)

Lesson 97 Name:

Father

commend

hands

spirit

122 Horizons® Penmanship Grade 1

Lesson 98 Name:

Father, into

your hands

I commend

my Spirit.

Horizons® Penmanship Grade 1 123

Lessons 99-100 - Bible Verse Practice & Special Page

Teaching Tips:

1. Do warm-up activities and review the meaning of the Bible verse.
2. On these pages the children will not only practice the Bible verse but will have the opportunity to show their best work on a special page that they can take home or display in the classroom.
3. Have the children take their time. Emphasize the spacing needed between words and make sure they include all necessary punctuation.
4. Encourage the children to stop if their hands become tired and rest for a minute.
5. Allow them to further decorate the pages if they choose.
6. Talk about sharing God's Word with others. Stress the importance of being able to write to others about God and being able to share His Word with them.
7. Discuss ways in which the special page can be used.
8. Children requiring additional practice may use the practice pages duplicated from the masters located in the back of the *Teacher's Guide*.

Bible Verse Lessons 96-100:

"Father, into your hands I commend my Spirit." (Luke 23:46)

Lesson 101 - Review Letters Yy, Zz

Teaching Tips:

1. Review and individual practice for letters: **Yy**, **Zz**.
2. Talk about the name and the sound each letter makes. Note how each letter is formed.
3. Warm-up for each letter and check position.
4. Have the students trace and copy the letters while observing the position, formation, and spacing.
5. Discuss the meaning of the sentence if desired.
6. Give the children time to rest if needed.
7. Praise all efforts.
8. Circle the best attempt for each letter.
9. Children requiring additional practice may use the practice pages duplicated from the masters located in the back of the *Teacher's Guide*.

Bible Verse Lessons 101-105:

"Do not be afraid, for I know you are looking for Jesus,...He is not here; he is risen, just as he said." (Matthew 28:5–6)

Lesson 101 Name:

Yy Yy

Zz Zz

Matthew 28:5–6

Do not be afraid.

Horizons® Penmanship Grade 1 127

Lessons 102-103 - Bible Verse Practice

Teaching Tips:

1. Review **Matthew 28:5–6** with the students and discuss the meaning of the verses.
2. Practice words and spacing of words and phrases from the Bible verse for the week.
3. Warm-up and check position.
4. Have the students trace and copy the words while observing the position, formation, spacing and punctuation.
5. Point out the ellipse (**...**) in the verse and explain to the students that this punctuation is used to show that words or phrases have been left out of the quoted material.
6. Discuss the meaning of the sentence if desired.
7. Give the children time to rest if needed.
8. Children requiring additional practice may use the practice pages duplicated from the masters located in the back of the *Teacher's Guide*.
9. Praise all efforts.
10. Circle the best attempt for each word.

Bible Verse Lessons 101-105:

"Do not be afraid, for I know you are looking for Jesus,...He is not here; he is risen, just as he said." (Matthew 28:5–6)

Lesson 102 Name:

risen

Matthew

know

He is risen.

128 Horizons® Penmanship Grade 1

Lesson 103 Name:

looking

looking for Jesus

as He said

He is not here;

Horizons® Penmanship Grade 1 129

Lessons 104-105 - Bible Verse Practice & Special Page

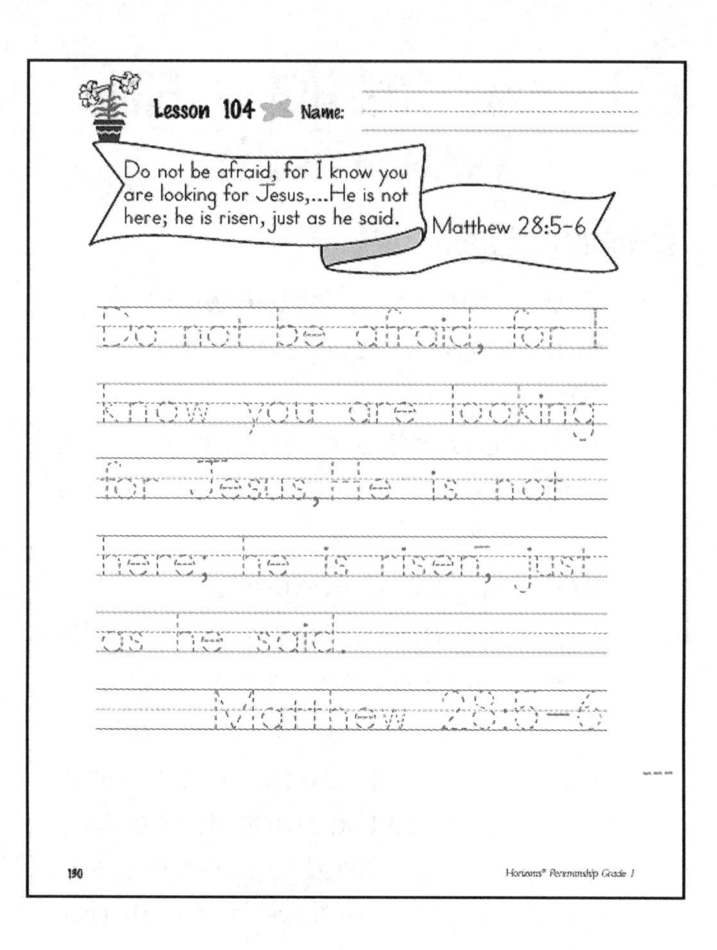

Teaching Tips:

1. Do warm-up activities and review the meaning of the Bible verse.
2. On these pages the children will not only practice the Bible verse but will have the opportunity to show their best work on a special page that they can take home or display in the classroom.
3. Have the children take their time. Emphasize the spacing needed between words and make sure they include all necessary punctuation.
4. Encourage the children to stop if their hands become tired and rest for a minute.
5. Allow them to further decorate the pages if they choose.
6. Talk about sharing God's Word with others. Stress the importance of being able to write to others about God and being able to share His Word with them.
7. Discuss ways in which the special page can be used.
8. Children requiring additional practice may use the practice pages duplicated from the masters located in the back of the *Teacher's Guide*.

Bible Verse Lessons 101-105:

"Do not be afraid, for I know you are looking for Jesus,...He is not here; he is risen, just as he said." (Matthew 28:5–6)

Lesson 106 - Review Letters Ll

Teaching Tips:

1. Review and individual practice for letters: **Ll**.
2. Talk about the name and the sound the letter makes. Note how the letter is formed.
3. Warm-up for each letter and check position.
4. Have the students trace and copy the letters and words while observing the position, formation, and spacing.
5. The two additional practice lines may be used for individual practice of letters or words that a student finds difficult. They may also be used for practicing a class sentence or a sentence created by the student.
6. Give the children time to rest if needed.
7. Praise all efforts.
8. Circle the best attempt for each letter or word.
9. Children requiring additional practice may use the practice pages duplicated from the masters located in the back of the *Teacher's Guide*.

Bible Verse Lessons 106-110:

"The Lord is my light and my salvation – whom shall I fear?" (Psalm 27:1)

Lesson 106 Name:

Ll Ll

my light

my salvation —

Horizons Penmanship Grade 1 133

Lessons 107-108 - Bible Verse & Sentence Writing Practice

Teaching Tips:

1. Review **Psalm 27:1** with the students and discuss the meaning of the verse.
2. Practice words and spacing of words and phrases from the Bible verse for the week.
3. Warm-up and check position.
4. Have the students trace and copy the words while observing the position, formation, spacing and punctuation.
5. Give the children time to rest if needed.
6. Children requiring additional practice may use the practice pages duplicated from the masters located in the back of the *Teacher's Guide*.
7. Praise all efforts.
8. Circle the best attempt for each word.
9. The extra lines in Lesson 108 are intended for a story based on the sentence. The story may be a group effort by the class or one created individually by the student.

Bible Verse Lessons 106-110:

"The Lord is my light and my salvation – whom shall I fear?" (Psalm 27:1)

Lesson 107 Name:

The Lord is my light.

The Lord is my salvation.

Whom shall I fear?

134 Horizons® Penmanship Grade 1

Lesson 108 Name:

The Lord is my life.

Horizons® Penmanship Grade 1 135

Lessons 109-110 - Bible Verse Practice & Special Page

Teaching Tips:

1. Do warm-up activities and review the meaning of the Bible verse.
2. On these pages the children will not only practice the Bible verse but will have the opportunity to show their best work on a special page that they can take home or display in the classroom.
3. Have the children take their time. Emphasize the spacing needed between words and make sure they include all necessary punctuation.
4. Encourage the children to stop if their hands become tired and rest for a minute.
5. Allow them to further decorate the pages if they choose.
6. Talk about sharing God's Word with others. Stress the importance of being able to write to others about God and being able to share His Word with them.
7. Discuss ways in which the special page can be used.
8. Children requiring additional practice may use the practice pages duplicated from the masters located in the back of the *Teacher's Guide*.

Bible Verse Lessons 106-110:

"The Lord is my light and my salvation – whom shall I fear?" (Psalm 27:1)

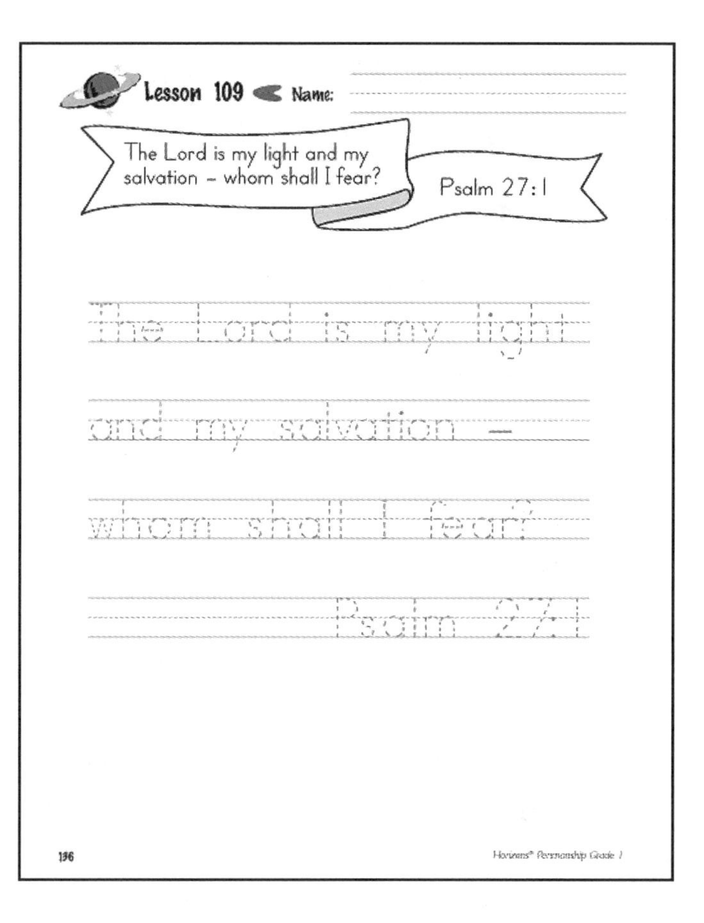

Lesson 111 - Bible Verse Practice

Teaching Tips:

1. Review **Psalm 100:1–2** with the students and discuss the meaning of the verses.
2. Practice words and spacing of words and phrases from the Bible verses for the week.
3. Warm-up and check position.
4. Have the students trace and copy the words while observing the position, formation, spacing and punctuation.
5. Give the children time to rest if needed.
6. Children requiring additional practice may use the practice pages duplicated from the masters located in the back of the *Teacher's Guide*.
7. Praise all efforts.
8. Circle the best attempt for each word.
9. The extra lines are to be used for practice of words that are difficult for the student, for sentence writing, for creative writing, or whatever use you deem helpful to the student's writing progress.

Bible Verse Lessons 111-115:

"Shout for joy to the Lord, all the earth. Worship the Lord with gladness; come before him with joyful songs." (Psalm 100:1–2)

Lesson 111 Name:

Psalm 100:1–2

Shout

worship

gladness

Horizons® Penmanship Grade 1 139

Lessons 112-113 - Bible Verse Practice

Teaching Tips:

1. Practice words and spacing of words and phrases from the Bible verses for the week.
2. Warm-up and check position.
3. Have the students trace and copy the words while observing the position, formation, spacing and punctuation.
4. Give the children time to rest if needed.
5. Children requiring additional practice may use the practice pages duplicated from the masters located in the back of the *Teacher's Guide*.
6. Praise all efforts.
7. Circle the best attempt for each word.
8. The extra lines are to be used for practice of words that are difficult for the student, for sentence writing, for creative writing, or whatever use you deem helpful to the student's writing progress.

Bible Verse Lessons 111-115:

"Shout for joy to the Lord, all the earth. Worship the Lord with gladness; come before him with joyful songs." (Psalm 100:1–2)

Lesson 112 Name:

Shout for joy.

Worship the Lord.

Come before him.

140 Horizons® Penmanship Grade 1

Lesson 113 Name:

Sing joyful songs.

Sing to the Lord.

Worship with gladness;

Horizons® Penmanship Grade 1 141

Lessons 114-115 - Bible Verse Practice & Special Page

Teaching Tips:

1. Do warm-up activities and review the meaning of the Bible verse.
2. On these pages the children will not only practice the Bible verse but will have the opportunity to show their best work on a special page that they can take home or display in the classroom.
3. Have the children take their time. Emphasize the spacing needed between words and make sure they include all necessary punctuation.
4. Encourage the children to stop if their hands become tired and rest for a minute.
5. Allow them to further decorate the pages if they choose.
6. Talk about sharing God's Word with others. Stress the importance of being able to write to others about God and being able to share His Word with them.
7. Discuss ways in which the special page can be used.
8. Children requiring additional practice may use the practice pages duplicated from the masters located in the back of the *Teacher's Guide*.

Bible Verse Lessons 111-115:

"Shout for joy to the Lord, all the earth. Worship the Lord with gladness; come before him with joyful songs." (Psalm 100:1–2)

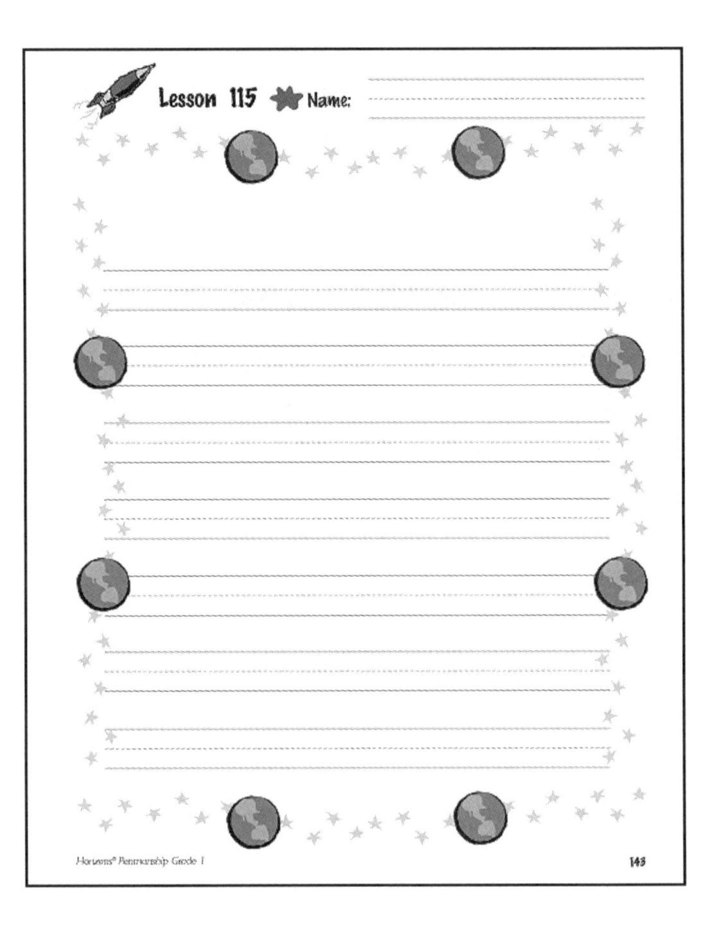

Lesson 116 - Bible Verse Practice

Teaching Tips:

1. Review **Psalm 100:3** with the students and discuss the meaning of the verses.
2. Practice words and spacing of words and phrases from the Bible verse for the week.
3. Warm-up and check position.
4. Have the students trace and copy the words while observing the position, formation, spacing and punctuation.
5. Give the children time to rest if needed.
6. Children requiring additional practice may use the practice pages duplicated from the masters located in the back of the *Teacher's Guide*.
7. Praise all efforts.
8. Circle the best attempt for each word.
9. The extra lines are to be used for practice of words that are difficult for the student, for sentence writing, for creative writing, or whatever use you deem helpful to the student's writing progress.

Bible Verse Lessons 116-120:

"Know that the Lord is God. It is he who made us, and we are his people, the sheep of this pasture." (Psalm 100:3)

Lesson 116 Name:

know

people

pasture

Horizons® Penmanship Grade 1 145

Lessons 117-118 - Bible Verse Practice

Teaching Tips:

1. Practice words and spacing of words and phrases from the Bible verse for the week.
2. Warm-up and check position.
3. Have the students trace and copy the words while observing the position, formation, spacing and punctuation.
4. Give the children time to rest if needed.
5. Children requiring additional practice may use the practice pages duplicated from the masters located in the back of the *Teacher's Guide*.
6. Praise all efforts.
7. Circle the best attempt for each word.
8. The extra lines are to be used for practice of words that are difficult for the student, for sentence writing, for creative writing, or whatever use you deem helpful to the student's writing progress.

Bible Verse Lessons 116-120:

"Know that the Lord is God. It is he who made us, and we are his people, the sheep of this pasture." (Psalm 100:3)

Lesson 117 Name:

The Lord is God.

He made us.

We are his people.

146 Horizons® Penmanship Grade 1

Lesson 118 Name:

We are like his sheep.

We rest in his pasture.

He is our shepherd.

Horizons® Penmanship Grade 1 147

Lessons 119-120 - Bible Verse Practice & Special Page

Teaching Tips:

1. Do warm-up activities and review the meaning of the Bible verse.
2. On these pages the children will not only practice the Bible verse but will have the opportunity to show their best work on a special page that they can take home or display in the classroom.
3. Have the children take their time. Emphasize the spacing needed between words and make sure they include all necessary punctuation.
4. Encourage the children to stop if their hands become tired and rest for a minute.
5. Allow them to further decorate the pages if they choose.
6. Talk about sharing God's Word with others. Stress the importance of being able to write to others about God and being able to share His Word with them.
7. Discuss ways in which the special page can be used.
8. Children requiring additional practice may use the practice pages duplicated from the masters located in the back of the *Teacher's Guide*.

Bible Verse Lessons 116-120:

"Know that the Lord is God. It is he who made us, and we are his people, the sheep of this pasture." (Psalm 100:3)

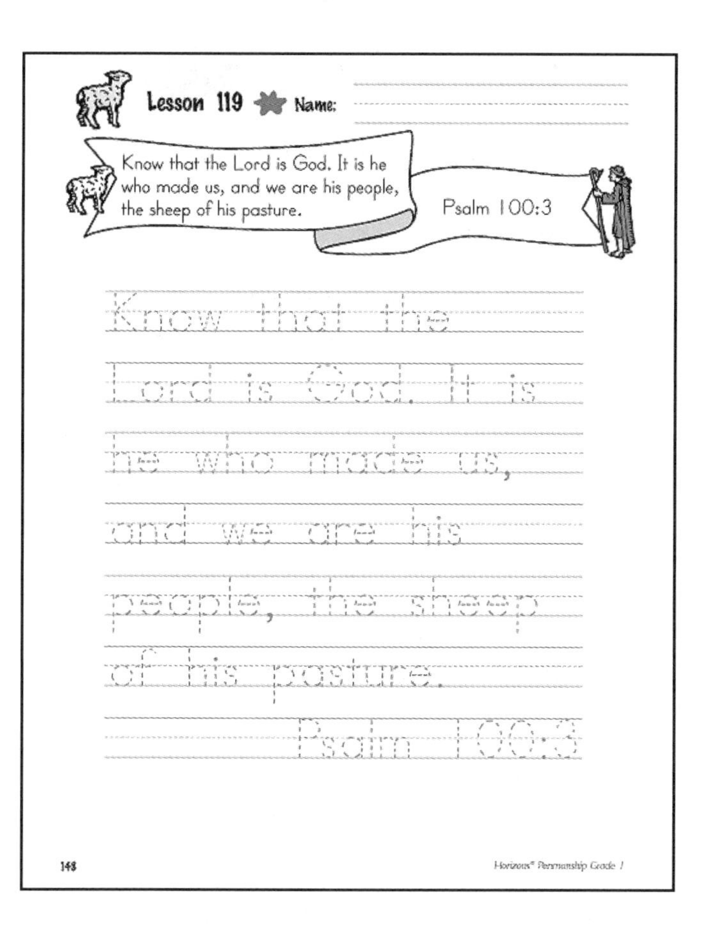

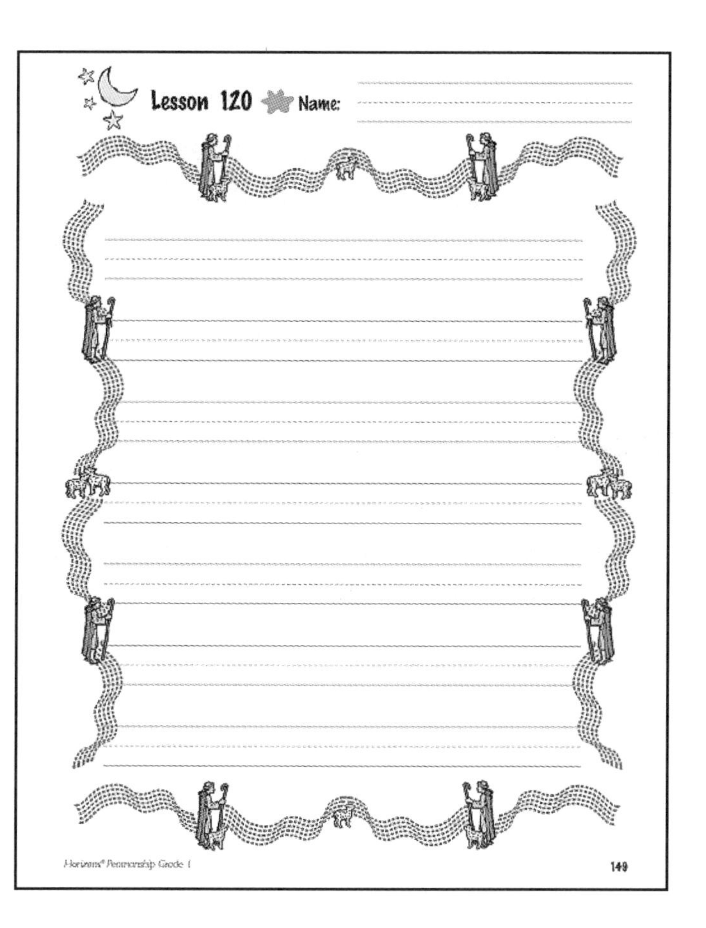

Lesson 121 - Bible Verse Practice

Teaching Tips:

1. Review **Psalm 100:4** with the students and discuss the meaning of the verses.
2. Practice words and spacing of words and phrases from the Bible verse for the week.
3. Warm-up and check position.
4. Have the students trace and copy the words while observing the position, formation, spacing and punctuation.
5. Give the children time to rest if needed.
6. Children requiring additional practice may use the practice pages duplicated from the masters located in the back of the *Teacher's Guide*.
7. Praise all efforts.
8. Circle the best attempt for each word.
9. The extra lines are to be used for practice of words that are difficult for the student, for sentence writing, for creative writing, or whatever use you deem helpful to the student's writing progress.

Bible Verse Lessons 121-125:

"Enter his gates with thanksgiving and his courts with praise; give thanks to him and praise his name." (Psalm 100:4)

Lesson 121 Name:

Enter

gates

thanksgiving

Horizons® Penmanship Grade 1 151

Lessons 122-123 - Bible Verse Practice

Teaching Tips:

1. Practice words and spacing of words and phrases from the Bible verse for the week.
2. Warm-up and check position.
3. Have the students trace and copy the words while observing the position, formation, spacing and punctuation.
4. Give the children time to rest if needed.
5. Children requiring additional practice may use the practice pages duplicated from the masters located in the back of the *Teacher's Guide*.
6. Praise all efforts.
7. Circle the best attempt for each word.
8. The extra lines are to be used for practice of words that are difficult for the student, for sentence writing, for creative writing, or whatever use you deem helpful to the student's writing progress.

Bible Verse Lessons 121-125:

"Enter his gates with thanksgiving and his courts with praise; give thanks to him and praise his name." (Psalm 100:4)

Lesson 122 Name:

courts

praise

Give thanks to him.

152 Horizons® Penmanship Grade 1

Lesson 123 Name:

Praise his name.

Enter his gates

with thanksgiving.

Horizons® Penmanship Grade 1 153

Lessons 124-125 - Bible Verse Practice & Special Page

Teaching Tips:

1. Do warm-up activities and review the meaning of the Bible verse.
2. On these pages the children will not only practice the Bible verse but will have the opportunity to show their best work on a special page that they can take home or display in the class-room.
3. Have the children take their time. Emphasize the spacing needed between words and make sure they include all necessary punctuation.
4. Encourage the children to stop if their hands become tired and rest for a minute.
5. Allow them to further decorate the pages if they choose.
6. Talk about sharing God's Word with others. Stress the importance of being able to write to others about God and being able to share His Word with them.
7. Discuss ways in which the special page can be used.
8. Children requiring additional practice may use the practice pages duplicated from the masters located in the back of the *Teacher's Guide*.

Bible Verse Lessons 121-125:

"Enter his gates with thanksgiving and his courts with praise; give thanks to him and praise his name." (Psalm 100:4)

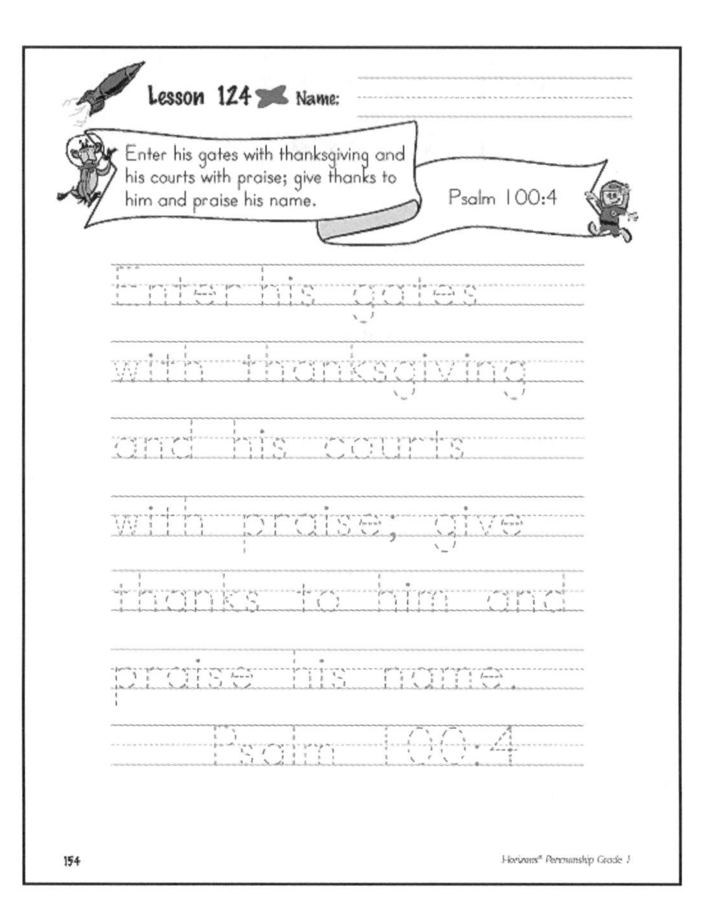

Lesson 126 - Bible Verse Practice

Teaching Tips:

1. Review **Psalm 100:5** with the students and discuss the meaning of the verse.
2. Practice words and spacing of words and phrases from the Bible verse for the week.
3. Warm-up and check position.
4. Have the students trace and copy the words while observing the position, formation, spacing and punctuation.
5. Give the children time to rest if needed.
6. Children requiring additional practice may use the practice pages duplicated from the masters located in the back of the *Teacher's Guide*.
7. Praise all efforts.
8. Circle the best attempt for each word.
9. The extra lines are to be used for practice of words that are difficult for the student, for sentence writing, for creative writing, or whatever use you deem helpful to the student's writing progress.

Bible Verse Lessons 126-130:

"For the Lord is good and his love endures forever; his faithfulness continues through all generations." (Psalm 100:5)

Lesson 126 Name:

endures

forever

faithfulness

Horizons® Penmanship Grade 1 157

Lessons 127-128 - Bible Verse Practice

Teaching Tips:

1. Practice words and spacing of words and phrases from the Bible verse for the week.
2. Warm-up and check position.
3. Have the students trace and copy the words while observing the position, formation, spacing and punctuation.
4. Discuss the meaning of the sentences if desired.
5. Give the children time to rest if needed.
6. Children requiring additional practice may use the practice pages duplicated from the masters located in the back of the *Teacher's Guide*.
7. Praise all efforts.
8. Circle the best attempt for each word.
9. The extra lines are to be used for practice of words that are difficult for the student, for sentence writing, for creative writing, or whatever use you deem helpful to the student's writing progress.

Bible Verse Lessons 126-130:

"For the Lord is good and his love endures forever; his faithfulness continues through all generations." (Psalm 100:5)

Lesson 127 Name:

continues

generations

through

158 Horizons® Penmanship Grade 1

Lesson 128 Name:

The Lord is good.

His love endures forever.

He is faithful.

Horizons® Penmanship Grade 1 159

Lessons 129-130 - Bible Verse Practice & Special Page

Teaching Tips:

1. Do warm-up activities and review the meaning of the Bible verse.
2. On these pages the children will not only practice the Bible verse but will have the opportunity to show their best work on a special page that they can take home or display in the classroom.
3. Have the children take their time. Emphasize the spacing needed between words and make sure they include all necessary punctuation.
4. Encourage the children to stop if their hands become tired and rest for a minute.
5. Allow them to further decorate the pages if they choose.
6. Talk about sharing God's Word with others. Stress the importance of being able to write to others about God and being able to share His Word with them.
7. Discuss ways in which the special page can be used.
8. Children requiring additional practice may use the practice pages duplicated from the masters located in the back of the *Teacher's Guide*.

Bible Verse Lessons 126-130:

"For the Lord is good and his love endures forever; his faithfulness continues through all generations." (Psalm 100:5)

Lesson 131 - Bible Verse Practice

Teaching Tips:

1. The next group of lessons focuses attention on the Lord's Prayer found in Matthew 6:9–13.
   Review **Matthew 6:9** and discuss the meaning of the verse and any unfamiliar words.
2. Practice capital and lowercase letters **Aa** through **Ee**.
3. Practice words and spacing of words and phrases from the Bible verse for the week.
4. Warm-up and check position.
5. Have the students trace and copy the words while observing the position, formation, spacing and punctuation.
6. Give the children time to rest if needed.
7. Children requiring additional practice may use the practice pages duplicated from the masters located in the back of the *Teacher's Guide*.
8. Praise all efforts.
9. Circle the best attempt for each word.
10. The extra lines are to be used for practice of words that are difficult for the student, for sentence writing, for creative writing, or whatever use you deem helpful to the student's writing progress.

Bible Verse Lessons 131-135:

"Our Father in heaven, hallowed be your name." (Matthew 6:9)

Lesson 131 Name:

Aa Bb Cc Dd Ee

Father

Heaven

Horizons® Penmanship Grade 1 163

Lessons 132-133 - Bible Verse Practice

Teaching Tips:

1. Practice words and spacing of words and phrases from the Bible verse for the week.
2. Warm-up and check position.
3. Have the students trace and copy the words while observing the position, formation, spacing and punctuation.
4. Discuss the meaning of the sentences if desired.
5. Give the children time to rest if needed.
6. Children requiring additional practice may use the practice pages duplicated from the masters located in the back of the *Teacher's Guide*.
7. Praise all efforts.
8. Circle the best attempt for each word.
9. The extra lines are to be used for practice of words that are difficult for the student, for sentence writing, for creative writing, or whatever use you deem helpful to the student's writing progress.

Bible Verse Lessons 131-135:

"Our Father in heaven, hallowed be your name." (Matthew 6:9)

Lesson 132 Name:

hallowed

name

Our Father

164 Horizons® Penmanship Grade 1

Lesson 133 Name:

Father in heaven

Holy is your name.

You are our Father.

Horizons® Penmanship Grade 1 165

Lessons 134-135 - Bible Verse Practice & Special Page

Teaching Tips:

1. Do warm-up activities and review the meaning of the Bible verse.
2. On these pages the children will not only practice the Bible verse but will have the opportunity to show their best work on a special page that they can take home or display in the classroom.
3. Have the children take their time. Emphasize the spacing needed between words and make sure they include all necessary punctuation.
4. Encourage the children to stop if their hands become tired and rest for a minute.
5. Allow them to further decorate the pages if they choose.
6. Talk about sharing God's Word with others. Stress the importance of being able to write to others about God and being able to share His Word with them.
7. Discuss ways in which the special page can be used.
8. Children requiring additional practice may use the practice pages duplicated from the masters located in the back of the *Teacher's Guide*.

Bible Verse Lessons 131-135:

"Our Father in heaven, hallowed be your name." (Matthew 6:9)

Lesson 136 - Bible Verse Practice

Teaching Tips:

1. Review **Matthew 6:10** and discuss the meaning of the verse and any unfamiliar words.
2. Practice capital and lowercase letters **Ff** through **Jj**.
3. Practice words and spacing of words and phrases from the Bible verse for the week.
4. Warm-up and check position.
5. Have the students trace and copy the words while observing the position, formation, spacing and punctuation.
6. Give the children time to rest if needed.
7. Children requiring additional practice may use the practice pages duplicated from the masters located in the back of the *Teacher's Guide*.
8. Praise all efforts.
9. Circle the best attempt for each word.
10. The extra lines are to be used for practice of words that are difficult for the student, for sentence writing, for creative writing, or whatever use you deem helpful to the student's writing progress.

Bible Verse Lessons 136-140:

"Your kingdom come, your will be done on earth as it is in heaven." (Matthew 6:10)

Lesson 136 Name:

Ff Gg Hh Ii Jj

kingdom

will

Horizons® Penmanship Grade 1 169

Lessons 137-138 - Bible Verse Practice

Teaching Tips:

1. Practice words and spacing of words and phrases from the Bible verse for the week.
2. Warm-up and check position.
3. Have the students trace and copy the words while observing the position, formation, spacing and punctuation.
4. Discuss the meaning of the sentences if desired.
5. Give the children time to rest if needed.
6. Children requiring additional practice may use the practice pages duplicated from the masters located in the back of the *Teacher's Guide*.
7. Praise all efforts.
8. Circle the best attempt for each word.
9. The extra lines are to be used for practice of words that are difficult for the student, for sentence writing, for creative writing, or whatever use you deem helpful to the student's writing progress.

Bible Verse Lessons 136-140:

"Your kingdom come, your will be done on earth as it is in heaven." (Matthew 6:10)

Lesson 137 Name:

earth

Your kingdom come.

Your will be done.

170 Horizons® Penmanship Grade 1

Lesson 138 Name:

on earth

as it is in heaven

Horizons® Penmanship Grade 1 171

Lessons 139-140 - Bible Verse Practice & Special Page

Teaching Tips:

1. Do warm-up activities and review the meaning of the Bible verse.
2. On these pages the children will not only practice the Bible verse but will have the opportunity to show their best work on a special page that they can take home or display in the classroom.
3. Have the children take their time. Emphasize the spacing needed between words and make sure they include all necessary punctuation.
4. Encourage the children to stop if their hands become tired and rest for a minute.
5. Allow them to further decorate the pages if they choose.
6. Talk about sharing God's Word with others. Stress the importance of being able to write to others about God and being able to share His Word with them.
7. Discuss ways in which the special page can be used.
8. Children requiring additional practice may use the practice pages duplicated from the masters located in the back of the *Teacher's Guide*.

Bible Verse Lessons 136-140:

"Your kingdom come, your will be done on earth as it is in heaven." (Matthew 6:10)

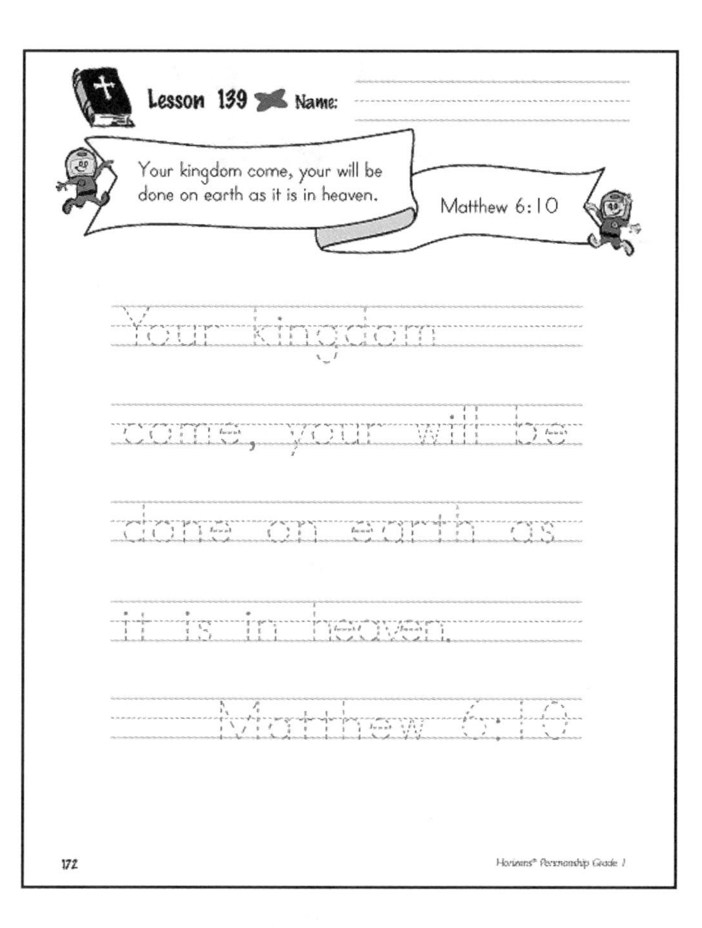

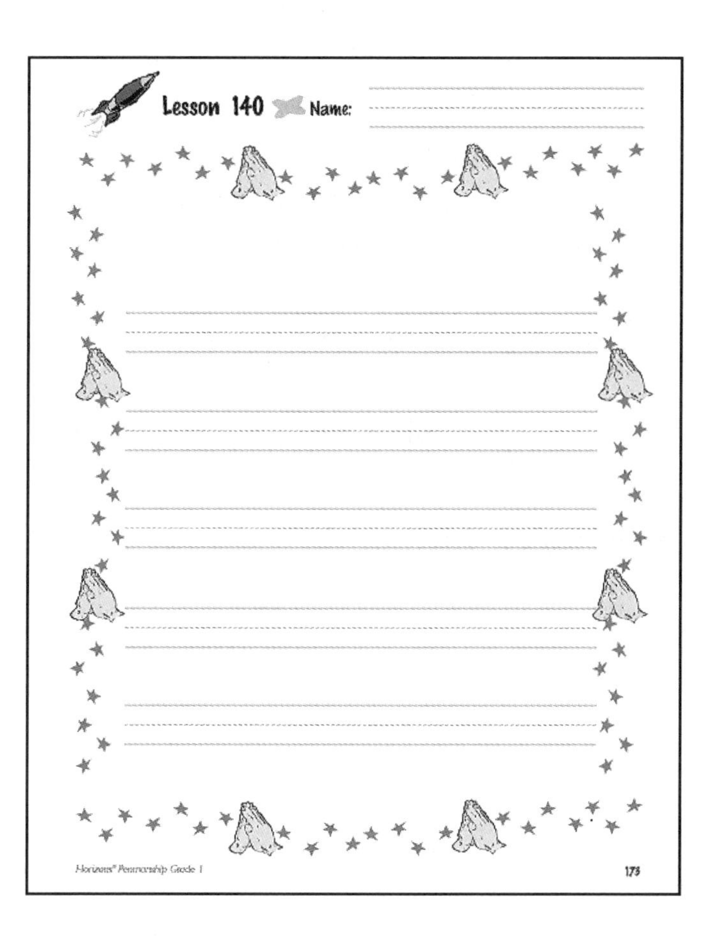

Lesson 141 - Bible Verse Practice

Teaching Tips:

1. Review **Matthew 6:11** and discuss the meaning of the verse and any unfamiliar words.
2. Practice capital and lowercase letters **Kk** through **Oo**.
3. Practice words and spacing of words and phrases from the Bible verse for the week.
4. Warm-up and check position.
5. Have the students trace and copy the words while observing the position, formation, spacing and punctuation.
6. Give the children time to rest if needed.
7. Children requiring additional practice may use the practice pages duplicated from the masters located in the back of the *Teacher's Guide*.
8. Praise all efforts.
9. Circle the best attempt for each word.
10. The extra lines are to be used for practice of words that are difficult for the student, for sentence writing, for creative writing, or whatever use you deem helpful to the student's writing progress.

Bible Verse Lessons 141-145:

"Give us today our daily bread."
(Matthew 6:11)

Lesson 141 Name:

Kk Ll Mm Nn Oo

Give

bread

Horizons® Penmanship Grade 1 175

Lessons 142-143 - Bible Verse Practice

Teaching Tips:

1. Practice words and spacing of words and phrases from the Bible verse for the week.
2. Warm-up and check position.
3. Have the students trace and copy the words while observing the position, formation, spacing and punctuation.
4. Discuss the meaning of the sentences if desired.
5. Give the children time to rest if needed.
6. Children requiring additional practice may use the practice pages duplicated from the masters located in the back of the *Teacher's Guide*.
7. Praise all efforts.
8. Circle the best attempt for each word.
9. The extra lines in **Lesson 143** are for the class to write a story or prayer, or the individual student may write a story or prayer of his or her own.

Bible Verse Lessons 141-145:

"Give us today our daily bread."
(Matthew 6:11)

Lesson 142 Name:

daily

Give God praise.

Give us our daily bread.

176 Horizons® Penmanship Grade 1

Lesson 143 Name:

Give us today

your blessing.

Horizons® Penmanship Grade 1 177

Lessons 144-145 - Bible Verse Practice & Special Page

Teaching Tips:

1. Do warm-up activities and review the meaning of the Bible verse.
2. On these pages the children will not only practice the Bible verse but will have the opportunity to show their best work on a special page that they can take home or display in the classroom.
3. Have the children take their time. Emphasize the spacing needed between words and make sure they include all necessary punctuation.
4. Encourage the children to stop if their hands become tired and rest for a minute.
5. Allow them to further decorate the pages if they choose.
6. Talk about sharing God's Word with others. Stress the importance of being able to write to others about God and being able to share His Word with them.
7. Discuss ways in which the special page can be used.
8. Children requiring additional practice may use the practice pages duplicated from the masters located in the back of the *Teacher's Guide*.

Bible Verse Lessons 141-145:

"Give us today our daily bread."
(Matthew 6:11)

Lesson 146 - Bible Verse Practice

Teaching Tips:

1. Review **Matthew 6:12** and discuss the meaning of the verse and any unfamiliar words.
2. Practice capital and lowercase letters **Pp** through **Tt**.
3. Practice words and spacing of words and phrases from the Bible verse for the week.
4. Warm-up and check position.
5. Have the students trace and copy the words while observing the position, formation, spacing and punctuation.
6. Give the children time to rest if needed.
7. Children requiring additional practice may use the practice pages duplicated from the masters located in the back of the *Teacher's Guide*.
8. Praise all efforts.
9. Circle the best attempt for each word.
10. The extra lines are to be used for practice of words that are difficult for the student, for sentence writing, for creative writing, or whatever use you deem helpful to the student's writing progress.

Bible Verse Lessons 146-150:

"Forgive us our debts, as we also have forgiven our debtors." (Matthew 6:12)

Lesson 146 Name:

Pp Qq Rr Ss Tt

Forgive

debts

Horizons® Penmanship Grade 1 131

Lessons 147-148 - Bible Verse Practice

Teaching Tips:

1. Practice words and spacing of words and phrases from the Bible verse for the week.
2. Warm-up and check position.
3. Have the students trace and copy the words while observing the position, formation, spacing and punctuation.
4. Discuss the meaning of the sentences if desired.
5. Give the children time to rest if needed.
6. Children requiring additional practice may use the practice pages duplicated from the masters located in the back of the *Teacher's Guide*.
7. Praise all efforts.
8. Circle the best attempt for each word.
9. The extra lines are to be used for practice of words that are difficult for the student, for sentence writing, for creative writing, or whatever use you deem helpful to the student's writing progress.

Bible Verse Lessons 146-150:

"Forgive us our debts, as we also have forgiven our debtors." (Matthew 6:12)

Lesson 147 Name:

forgiven

debtors

Forgive us.

182 Horizons® Penmanship Grade 1

Lesson 148 Name:

We forgive.

Father, forgive us.

Forgive us as we

also have forgiven.

Horizons® Penmanship Grade 1 183

Lessons 149-150 - Bible Verse Practice & Special Page

Teaching Tips:

1. Do warm-up activities and review the meaning of the Bible verse.
2. On these pages the children will not only practice the Bible verse but will have the opportunity to show their best work on a special page that they can take home or display in the classroom.
3. Have the children take their time. Emphasize the spacing needed between words and make sure they include all necessary punctuation.
4. Encourage the children to stop if their hands become tired and rest for a minute.
5. Allow them to further decorate the pages if they choose.
6. Talk about sharing God's Word with others. Stress the importance of being able to write to others about God and being able to share His Word with them.
7. Discuss ways in which the special page can be used.
8. Children requiring additional practice may use the practice pages duplicated from the masters located in the back of the *Teacher's Guide*.

Bible Verse Lessons 146-150:

"Forgive us our debts, as we also have forgiven our debtors." (Matthew 6:12)

Lesson 151 - Bible Verse Practice

Teaching Tips:

1. Review **Matthew 6:13** and discuss the meaning of the verse and any unfamiliar words.
2. Practice capital and lowercase letters **Uu** through **Zz**.
3. Practice words and spacing of words and phrases from the Bible verse for the week.
4. Warm-up and check position.
5. Have the students trace and copy the words while observing the position, formation, spacing and punctuation.
6. Give the children time to rest if needed.
7. Children requiring additional practice may use the practice pages duplicated from the masters located in the back of the *Teacher's Guide*.
8. Praise all efforts.
9. Circle the best attempt for each word.
10. The extra lines are to be used for practice of words that are difficult for the student, for sentence writing, for creative writing, or whatever use you deem helpful to the student's writing progress.

Lesson 151 Name:

Uu Vv Ww Xx Yy Zz

lead

temptation

Horizons® Penmanship Grade 1 187

Bible Verse Lessons 151-155:

"And lead us not into temptation, but deliver us from the evil one." (Matthew 6:13)

Lessons 152-153 - Bible Verse Practice

Teaching Tips:

1. Practice words and spacing of words and phrases from the Bible verse for the week.
2. Warm-up and check position.
3. Have the students trace and copy the words while observing the position, formation, spacing and punctuation.
4. Discuss the meaning of the sentences if desired.
5. Give the children time to rest if needed.
6. Children requiring additional practice may use the practice pages duplicated from the masters located in the back of the *Teacher's Guide*.
7. Praise all efforts.
8. Circle the best attempt for each word.
9. The extra lines are to be used for practice of words that are difficult for the student, for sentence writing, for creative writing, or whatever use you deem helpful to the student's writing progress.

Bible Verse Lessons 151-155:

"And lead us not into temptation, but deliver us from the evil one." (Matthew 6:13)

Lesson 152 Name:

deliver

evil

Deliver us from evil.

188 Horizons® Penmanship Grade 1

Lesson 153 Name:

Lead us away from evil.

Lead us not

into temptation.

Horizons® Penmanship Grade 1 189

Lessons 154-155 - Bible Verse Practice & Special Page

Teaching Tips:

1. Do warm-up activities and review the meaning of the Bible verse.
2. On these pages the children will not only practice the Bible verse but will have the opportunity to show their best work on a special page that they can take home or display in the classroom.
3. Have the children take their time. Emphasize the spacing needed between words and make sure they include all necessary punctuation.
4. Encourage the children to stop if their hands become tired and rest for a minute.
5. Allow them to further decorate the pages if they choose.
6. Talk about sharing God's Word with others. Stress the importance of being able to write to others about God and being able to share His Word with them.
7. Discuss ways in which the special page can be used.
8. Children requiring additional practice may use the practice pages duplicated from the masters located in the back of the *Teacher's Guide*.

Bible Verse Lessons 151-155:

"And lead us not into temptation, but deliver us from the evil one." (Matthew 6:13)

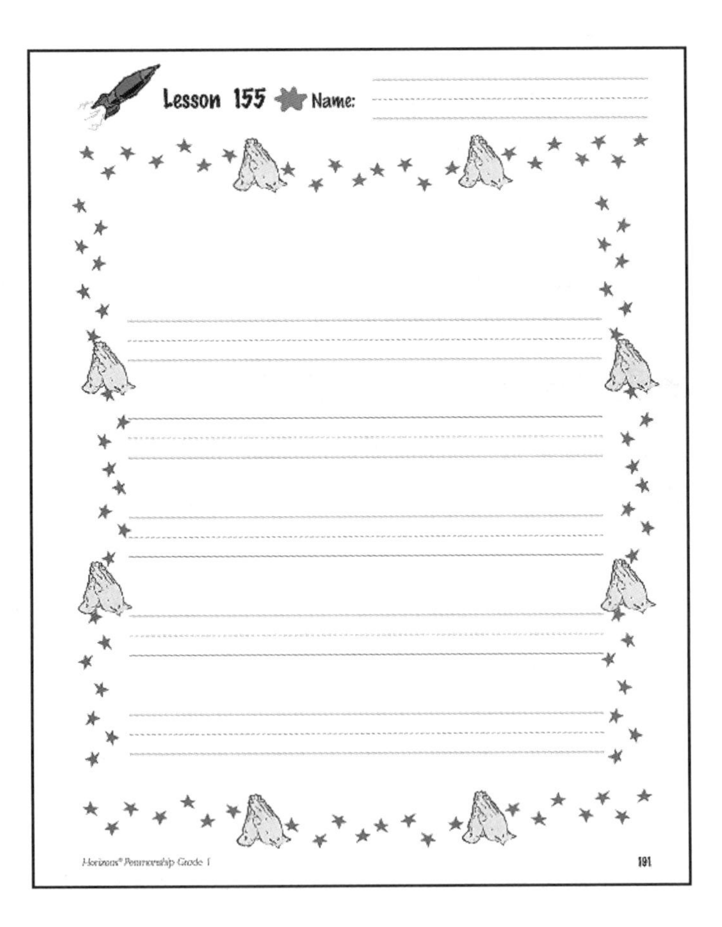

Lesson 156 - Capital Letter Practice

Teaching Tips:

1. Talk about the name and the sound each letter makes. Note how each letter is formed.
2. Warm-up for each letter and check position.
3. Have the students write all capital letters while observing the position, formation, and spacing.
4. Praise all efforts.
5. Circle the best attempt for each letter.

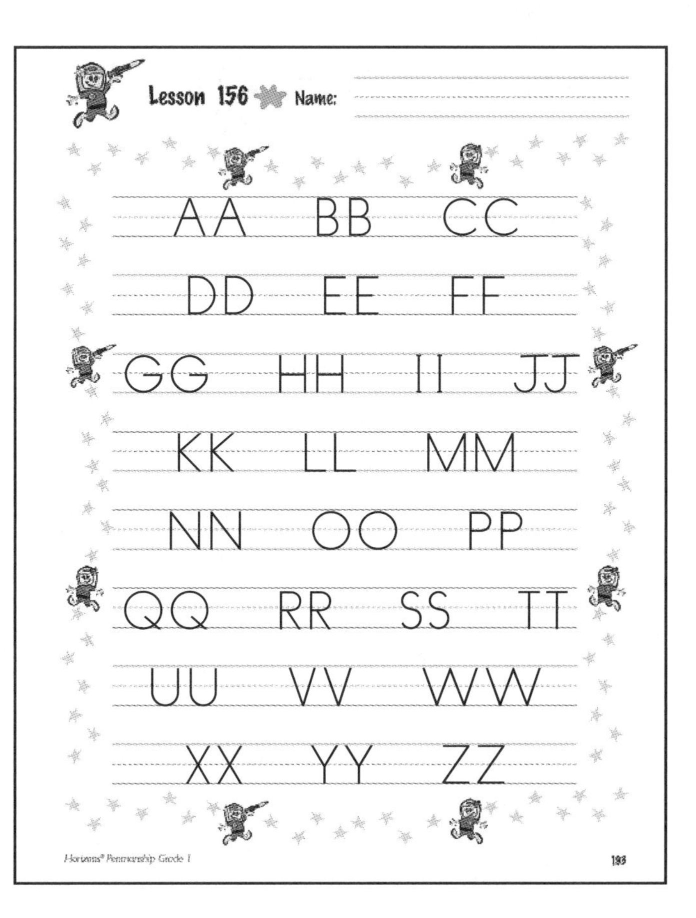

Lesson 156 Name:

AA BB CC

DD EE FF

GG HH II JJ

KK LL MM

NN OO PP

QQ RR SS TT

UU VV WW

XX YY ZZ

Horizons® Penmanship Grade 1 193

Lesson 157 - Lowercase Letter & Number Practice

Teaching Tips:

1. Talk about the name and the sound each letter makes. Note how each letter is formed.
2. Warm-up for each letter and check position.
3. Have the students write all lowercase letters and numbers 0–9 while observing the position, formation, and spacing of each.
4. Praise all efforts.
5. Circle the best attempt for each letter and number.

Lesson 157 Name:

aa bb cc dd

ee ff gg hh ii

jj kk ll mm

nn oo pp qq

rr ss tt uu vv

ww xx yy zz

1 2 3 4 5

6 7 8 9 0

194 Horizons® Penmanship Grade 1

Lesson 158 - Favorite Bible Verse

Teaching Tips:

1. Allow the student to select his/her favorite Bible verse from the year's work and copy it here.
2. Have the children take their time. Emphasize the spacing needed between words and make sure they include all necessary punctuation.
3. Encourage the children to stop if their hands become tired and rest for a minute.
4. Children requiring additional practice may use the practice pages duplicated from the masters located in the back of the *Teacher's Guide*.

Lesson 159 - Favorite Bible Verse

Teaching Tips:

1. The student may use this page to practice writing his/her own sentences. Encourage neatness and originality.
2. Have the children take their time. Emphasize the spacing needed between words and make sure they include all necessary punctuation.
3. Encourage the children to stop if their hands become tired and rest for a minute.
4. Children requiring additional practice may use the practice pages duplicated from the masters located in the back of the *Teacher's Guide*.

Lesson 160 - The Lord's Prayer

Teaching Tips:

1. Three pages are provided for the student to write the Lord's Prayer.
2. Emphasize the spacing needed between words and make sure they include all necessary punctuation.
3. Talk about sharing God's Word with others. Stress the importance of being able to write to others about God and being able to share His Word with them. Discuss ways in which these pages can be used.
4. Children requiring additional practice may use the practice pages duplicated from the masters located in the back of the *Teacher's Guide*.

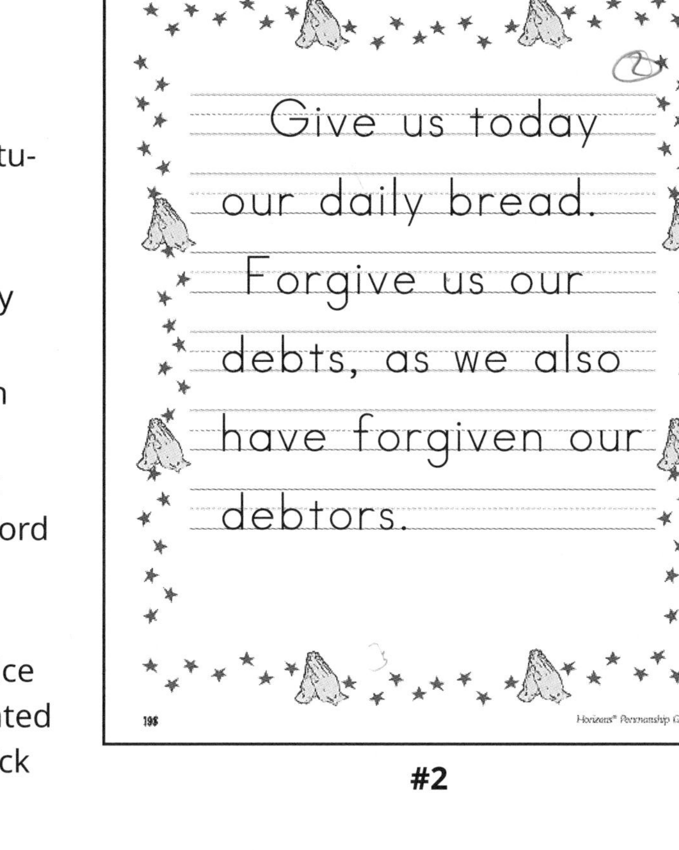

#2

#1

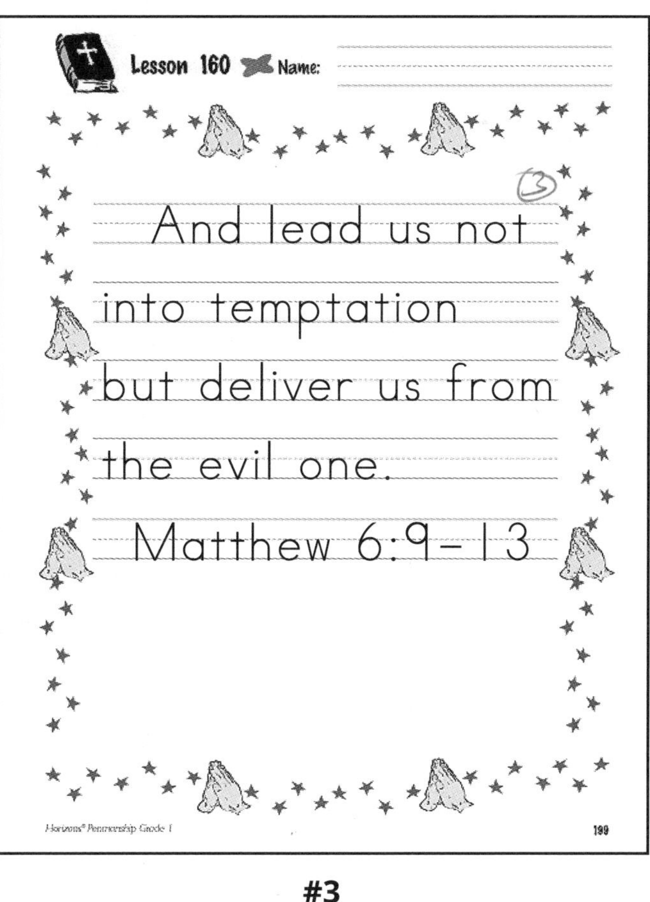

#3

Reproducible Practice Pages

Motor Skills Writing Practice

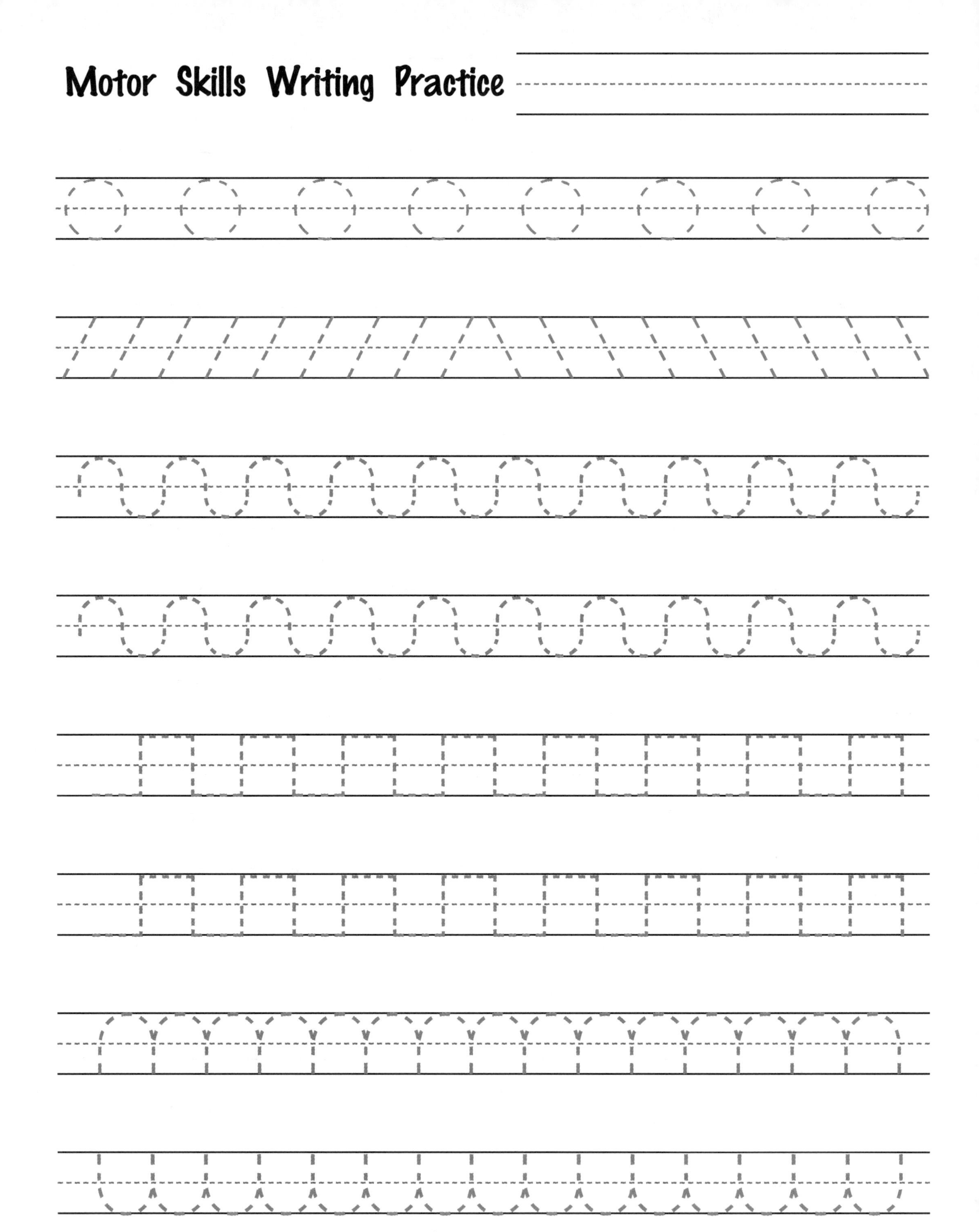

Motor Skills Writing Practice

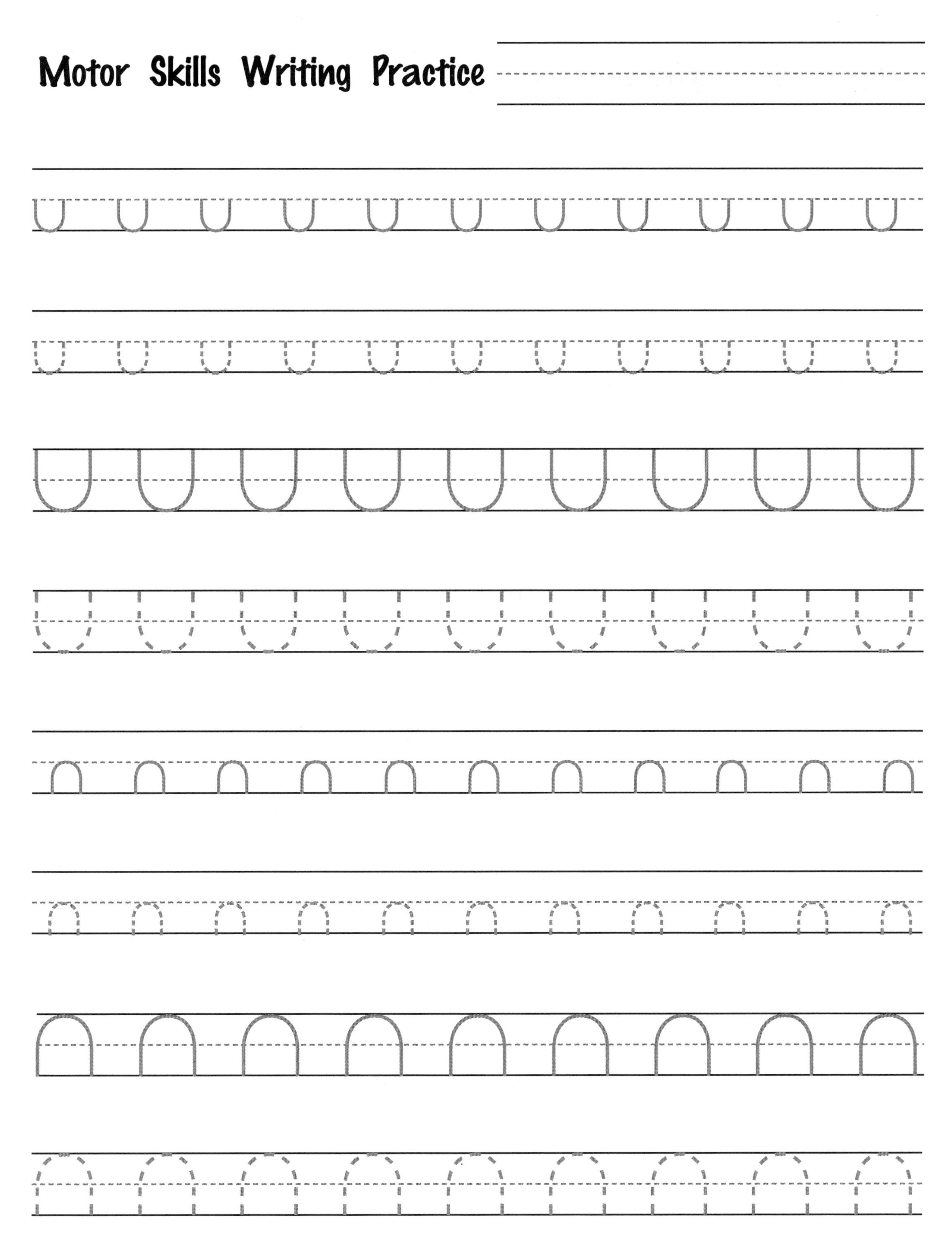

Motor Skills Writing Practice

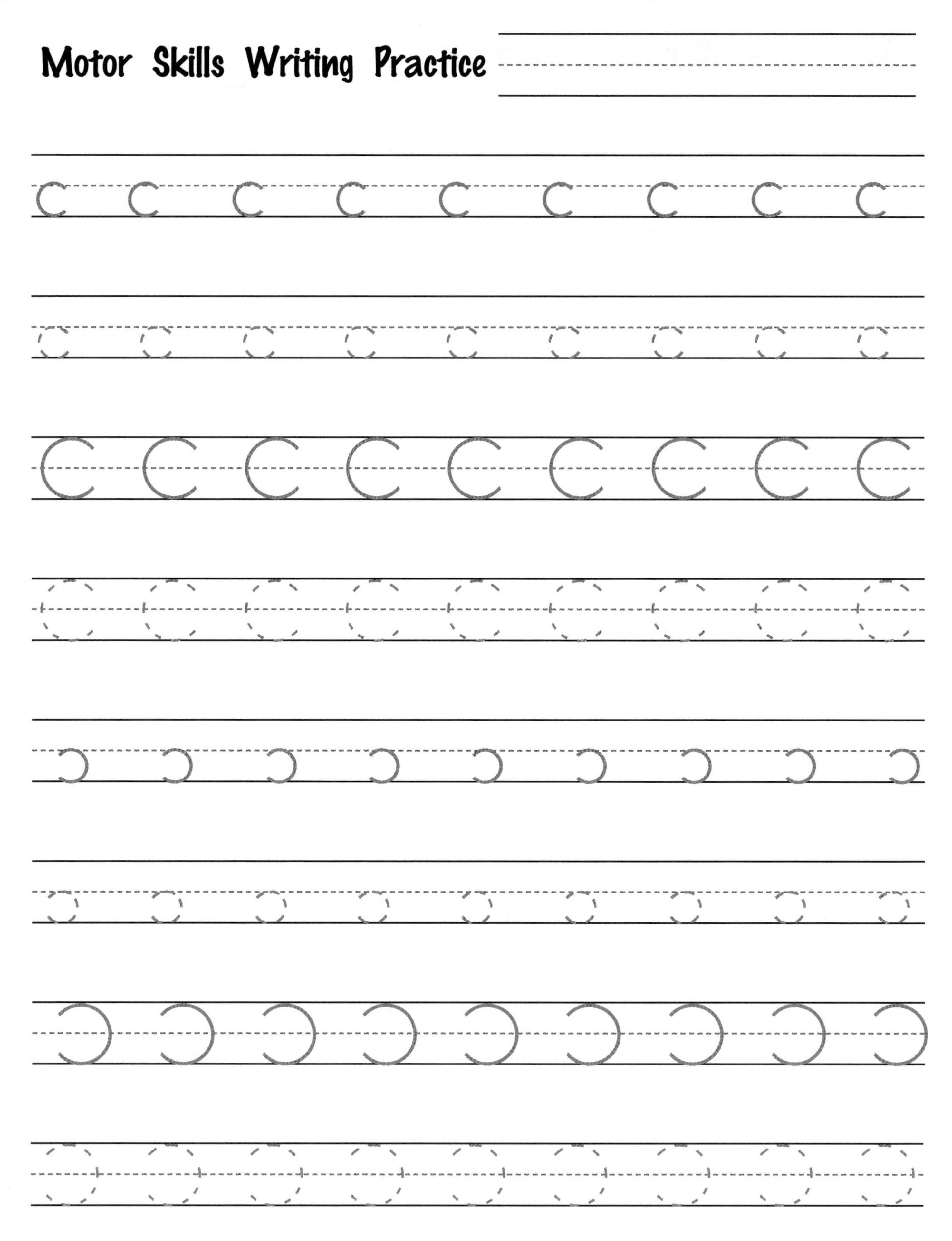

Lesson 40 Practice Page

Lesson 45 Practice Page

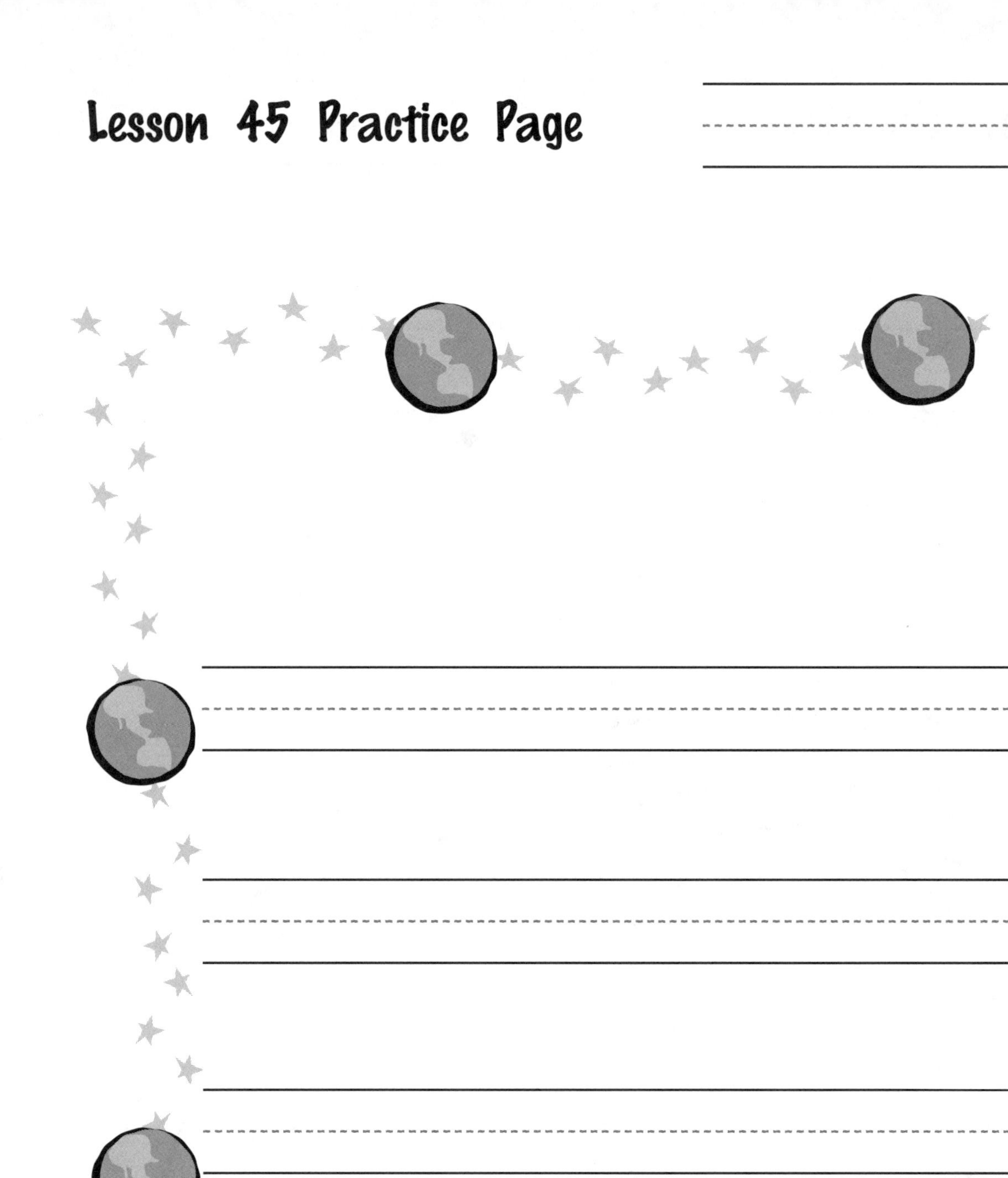

Lesson 50 Practice Page

Lesson 55 Practice Page

Lesson 60 Practice Page

Lesson 65 Practice Page

Lesson 70 Practice Page

Lesson 75 Practice Page

Lesson 80 Practice Page

Lesson 85 Practice Page

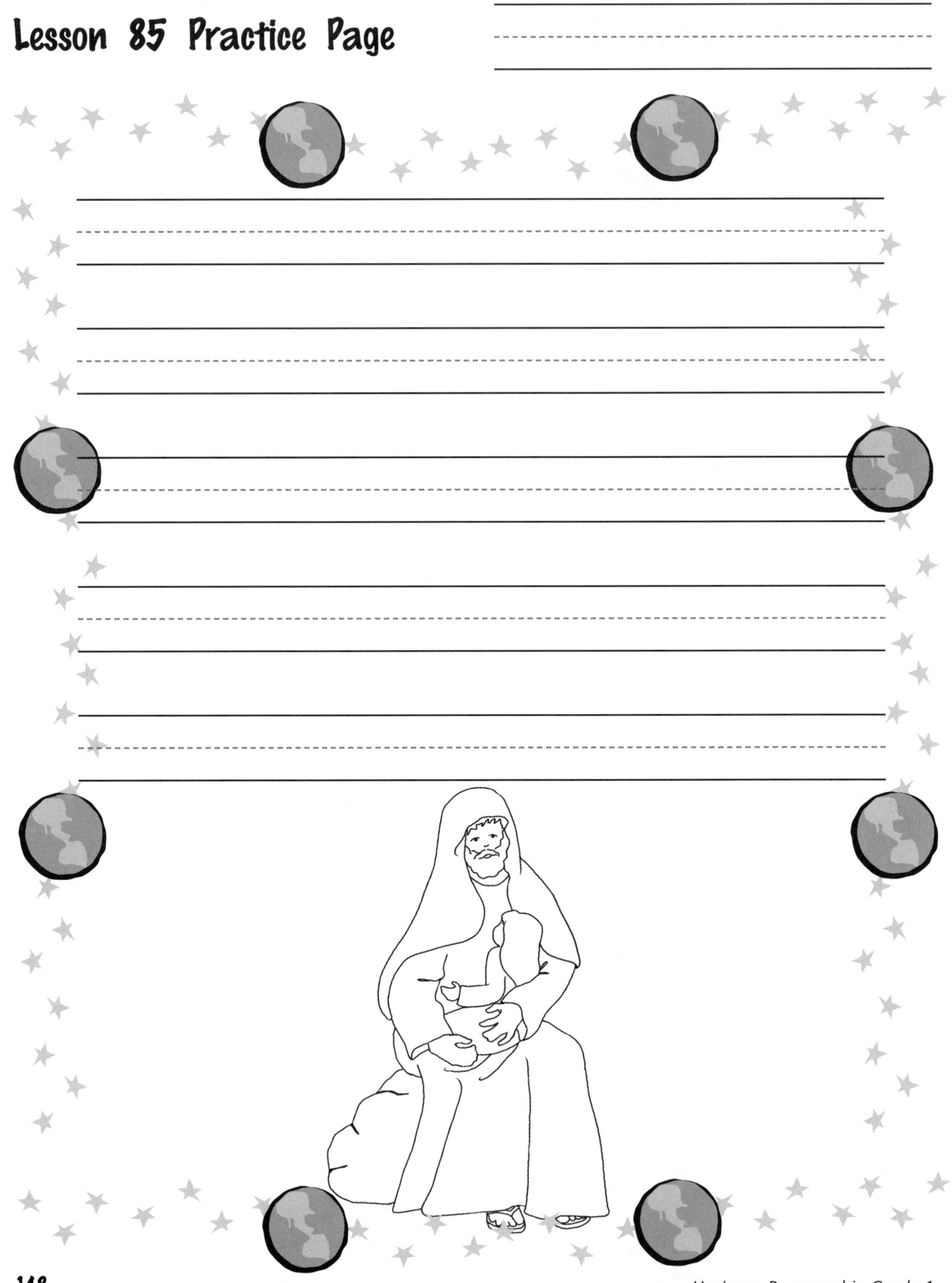

Lesson 90 Practice Page

Lesson 95 Practice Page

Lesson 100 Practice Page

Lesson 105 Practice Page

Lesson 110 Practice Page

Lesson 115 Practice Page

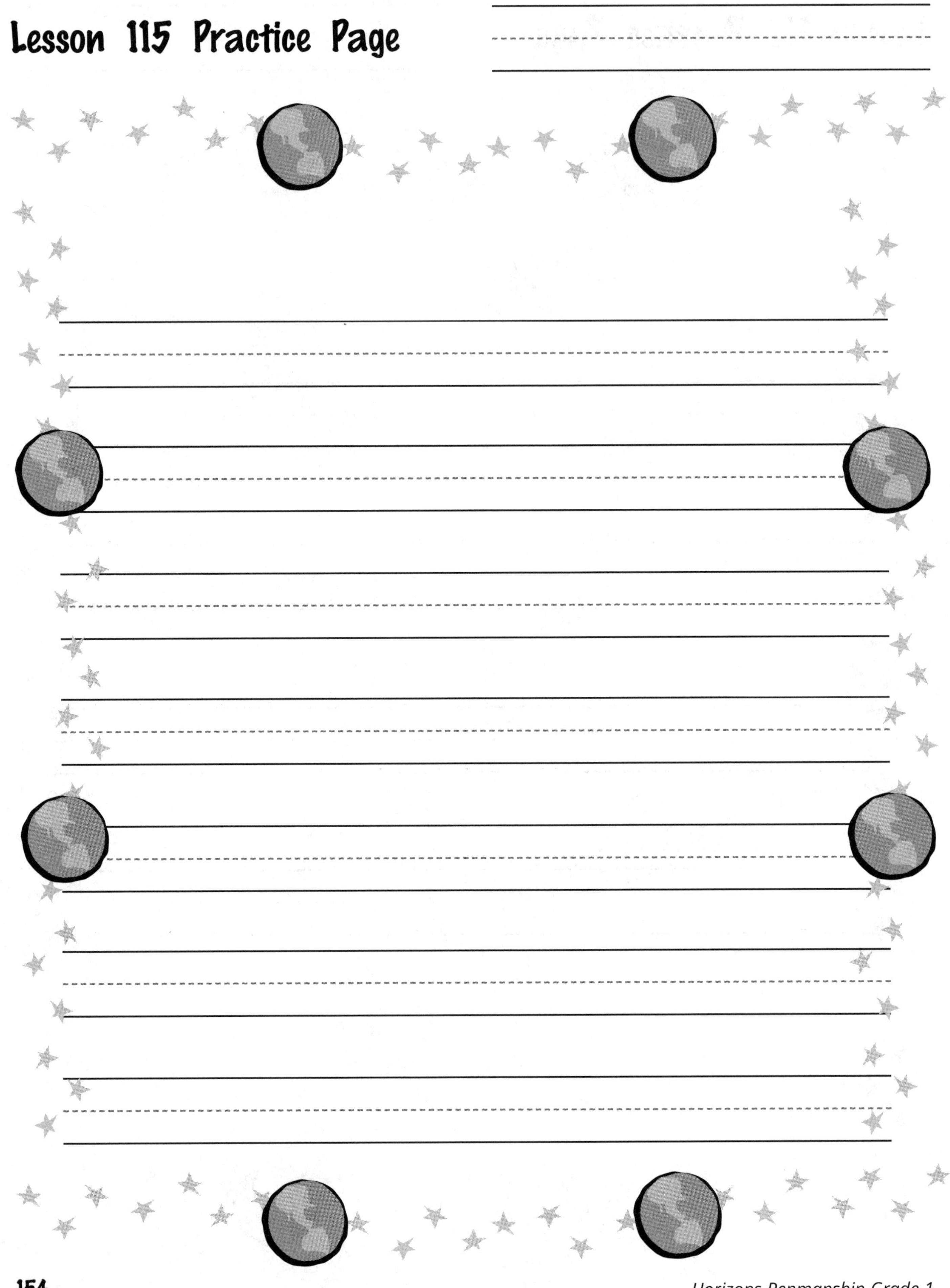

Lesson 120 Practice Page

Lesson 125 Practice Page

Lesson 130 Practice Page

Lesson 135 Practice Page

Lesson 140 Practice Page

Lesson 145 Practice Page

Lesson 150 Practice Page

Lesson 155 Practice Page

Lesson 156 Practice Page

Lesson 157 Practice Page

Lesson 158 Practice Page

Lesson 159 Practice Page

Lesson 160 Practice Page

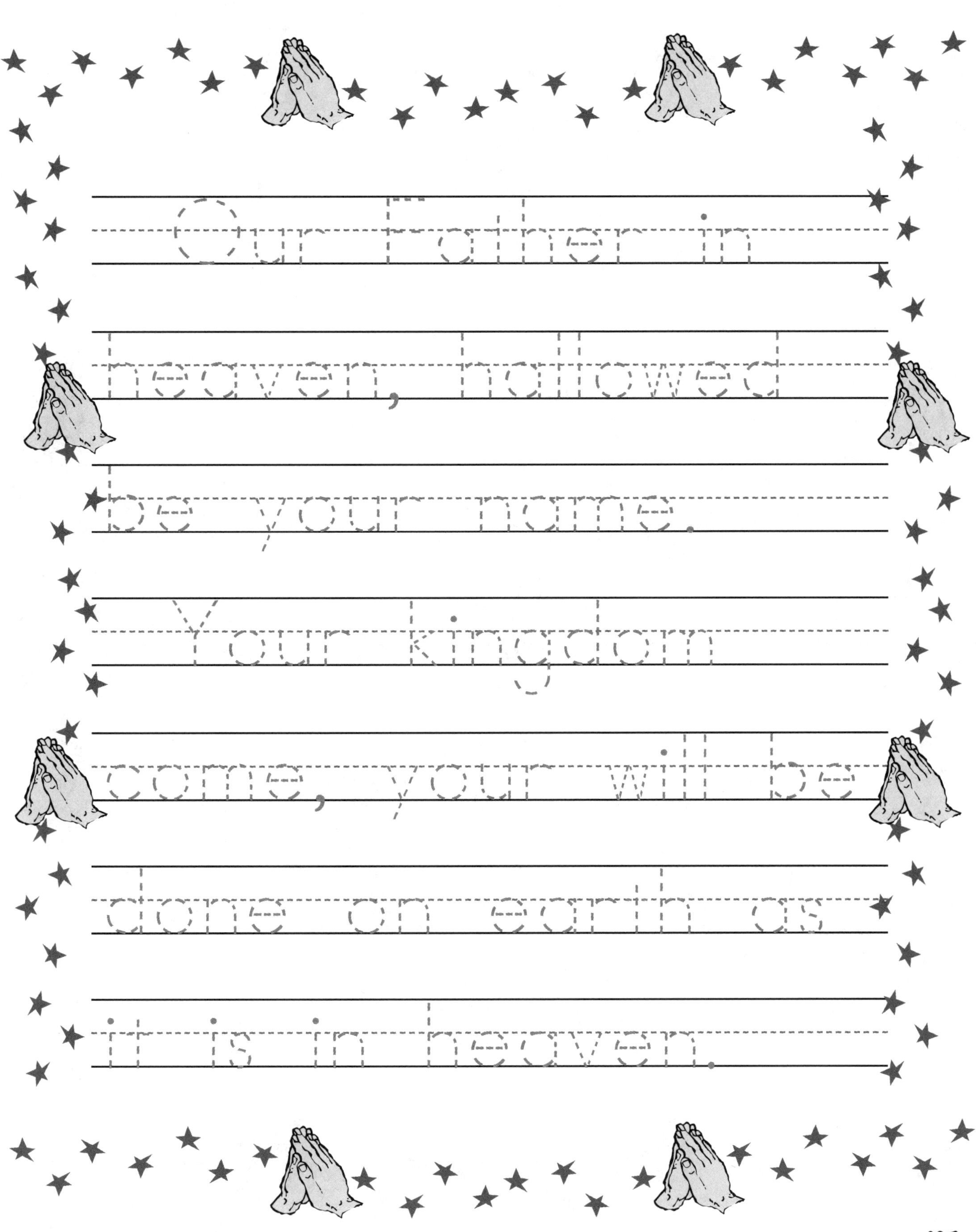

Lesson 160 Practice Page

Lesson 160 Practice Page